TUTORING WITH STUDENTS

a handbook for establishing
tutorial programs in schools

TUTORING WITH STUDENTS
a handbook for establishing tutorial programs in schools

RALPH J. MELARAGNO

EDUCATIONAL TECHNOLOGY PUBLICATIONS

ENGLEWOOD CLIFFS, NEW JERSEY 07632

Library of Congress Cataloging in Publication Data

Melaragno, Ralph J
    Tutoring with students.

    Bibliography: p.
    1. Tutors and tutoring—Handbooks, manuals, etc.
I. Title.
LC41.M44   371.39'4   75-40045
ISBN 0-87778-090-0

Printed in the United States of America.

Library of Congress Catalog Card Number: 75-40045.

International Standard Book Number: 0-87778-090-0.

First Printing: February, 1976.

Preface

This manual has been prepared for schools that have, in one way or another, heard about the Tutorial Community Program and have expressed an interest in learning how to put into operation a program like it. The audience for this manual should be large, judging by the number of people who have visited Tutorial Community schools in Los Angeles or have read about them and subsequently have asked for details.

Although most people who have requested the details have known something about the development of the program, a little needs to be said here about how the program came to be. This program is not a theoretical one that has been designed from someone's good ideas. Rather it has been developed gradually over a six-year period in elementary schools within the Los Angeles Unified School District. It has, then, stood the test of the realities of public education and is a viable program operating in not untypical public schools.

The research and development that went into the program was conducted by the Tutorial Community Project (TCP) under the sponsorship of The Ford Foundation. TCP had two objectives: the development of model innovative elementary schools characterized by individualized instruction through tutoring, shared planning and decision-making, and school-community interactions; and the development of dissemination procedures for spreading tutorial community concepts. This manual is part of the dissemination materials.

This book will be useful to school personnel who have considered initiating a tutorial program and desire specific guidance. Schools already implementing tutoring can use the ideas presented here to extend their programs. Schools of education may find the book appropriate for teacher-training courses in which tutoring is treated as a means of individualizing instruction and as a technique for promoting student-to-student interaction.

Many people played important parts in the development of the intergrade tutoring program presented in this manual. My colleague, Gerald Newmark, shared with me the directorship of TCP and was deeply involved with the development of intergrade tutoring; much of what appears in this manual came into being with his assistance. However, the approach to intergrade tutoring described here is strictly the author's responsibility.

Over a six-year period the staffs of Pacoima, Plainview, and Norwood Elementary Schools helped develop, evaluate, and revise intergrade tutoring. Quite simply, the program would never have reached its present state without them. Credit should go particularly to three tutoring coordinators: Floyd Cottam, Virginia Davis, and Barbara Teachenor.

Donald Watson was instrumental in assisting with the reduction of various fragmentary ideas to the written word. During the six years of development, Don worked closely with me in trying out ideas and, finally, in preparing this manual.

Probably most importantly my wife, Eddye, is responsible for the quality of what appears herein. As a skillful teacher, and as a consummate critic, she guaranteed that the final intergrade tutoring program would accomplish that for which it was designed.

Ralph J. Melaragno

October, 1975

Table of Contents

TUTORING WITH STUDENTS
a handbook for establishing
tutorial programs in schools

Introduction

"The saying, 'He who teaches others, teaches himself,' is very true, not only because constant repetition impresses a fact indelibly on the mind, but because the process of teaching in itself gives a deeper insight into the subject taught."

John Comenius
The Great Didactic

"The idea of students learning through helping each other is a very promising alternative to the traditional system of learning through competing with each other. It also makes the acquisition of knowledge and skills valuable, not in the service of competition for grades but as the means for personally significant interactions with others."

Herbert Thelen
"The Human Person Defined"

WHAT IS "INTERGRADE TUTORING"?

Perhaps the question to ask is, "After all that's already been said about children tutoring one another, and learning by teaching, what more is there to say?"

Or maybe the question really is, "How can all that makes up the process of older students tutoring younger ones be pulled together into a simple definition?"

Both questions are appropriate. So much has been written about tutoring—in journals, magazines, newspapers, books—that it's a challenge to find fresh or unique things to say. And the whole process of tutoring encompasses such a range of elements—schools, curriculum, instruction, education, human relations, teachers, administrators, parents, older tutors, younger learners—that it may defy definition.

One could begin by quoting educational philosophers who note that the most effective learning takes place when someone teaches something to someone else, and then describe tutoring as a prominent example of this process. Or one could start with the finding of child development specialists that most of what young children learn they learn from their peers, and indicate that tutoring capitalizes on peer learning. Or one could cite the social scientists' warnings about the increasing isolation of the individual, and point out that tutoring provides a helping relationship to overcome alienation. Any of these approaches would be valid, for all are true. Yet each lacks capturing completely the heart—or soul—of an intergrade tutoring program.

In simplest terms, intergrade tutoring means an older student tutoring a younger one. The intergrade tutoring program described in this book certainly means that, but it also means a great deal more. It means concerned adults—parents, teachers, administrators—working together for the betterment of students. It means teachers and student-tutors developing a spirit of colleagueship. It means students of all ages improving in their academic skills. It means students developing positive attitudes toward education, learning, school, other people, and themselves. And, it may mean the beginning of changing archaic and sterile academic institutions into viable, dynamic, and humane "communities."

As used in this manual, intergrade tutoring is a systematic approach to individualizing instruction, to upgrading achievement, and to fostering change and growth, in an elementary school. It's a carefully developed and tested sequence of activities for school-wide implementation of student tutoring. It's a whole new way of approaching education—successfully.

"It has long been obvious that children learn from their peers, but a more significant observation is that children learn more from teaching other children. From this a major educational strategy follows: namely, that every child must be given the opportunity to play the teaching role, because it is through playing this role that he may really learn how to learn."

> *Alan Gartner, Mary Kohler, Frank Riessman*
> **Children Teach Children**

THE VALUE OF INTERGRADE TUTORING

Today thousands of tutoring programs are being carried out in elementary schools in the United States. They range from casual pairings of a few students to an entire school involvement (as in Tutorial Community schools). In almost every case the people responsible for tutoring have tried to demonstrate the value of tutoring.

Many of the "evaluations" have taken the form of subjective reports, using testimonials of the benefits accruing from tutoring. Given the inadequacies of current evaluation procedures, that's understandable. However, there *are* instances of more rigorous approaches to evaluation which support a general conclusion: a healthy tutoring program results in improved academic achievement and more positive student feelings about school for both learners and tutors. Consider these examples:

- In New York City, high school students tutored elementary school students for five months. Younger learners averaged six months' reading improvement; older tutors averaged 3.4 years' reading improvement.

- In Ontario, California, junior high tutors worked with elementary school learners for seven months, while comparable students not involved in tutoring served as controls. The junior high tutors' reading scores exceeded controls' scores by three months, their math scores exceeded controls' by three months, and their language scores exceeded controls' by two months. The elementary learners' reading scores exceeded controls' by two months, and their language scores exceeded controls' by one month.

- In Los Angeles, fifth and sixth graders tutored kindergarteners for six weeks. Tutored kindergarteners learned significantly more than children who received no tutoring; they looked forward to tutoring and had an absence rate of almost zero.

Compared with older students who didn't tutor, the tutors showed significantly more positive attitudes, improved attendance, and better feelings about themselves.

- In American Fork, Utah, fourth and fifth graders tutored non-reading second graders for five months. The former non-reading learners scored 83 percent on a reading test, and parents of tutors and learners reported specific benefits to their children.

- At Pacoima Elementary School, Pacoima, California, fifth and sixth grade tutors worked with first and second grade learners for two and one-half months. Tutors' reading achievement rose five months, younger learners' reading achievement rose eight months, and both groups showed modest positive changes in attitude toward school.

"To be honest, I was amazed at how far my class came this year when I compared it with my other classes. I never made that much progress before, and I know it's because of the tutoring program."

Second Grade Teacher
Plainview Elementary School

"A regular tutoring program has done wonders for my kids. Some of them, whom I hadn't been able to reach, changed and started to succeed after they had been a tutor for a while."

Sixth Grade Teacher
Norwood Elementary School

In schools that have initiated intergrade tutoring programs, faculties consistently point out three features: (1) younger students receive more individual attention than could ever be possible in a conventional instructional setting; (2) older students sharpen and refine their own skills as they tutor younger students; and (3) all students become more interested in and enthusiastic about learning. Since most of these schools originally experienced chronic underachievement and low morale among students and teachers, observers have noted an added benefit: as teamwork and achievement improve, the general atmosphere permeating the school becomes more positive.

These, then, are the rewards of a successful tutoring program: First, there is the observable (and measurable) increase in achievement for all students involved. Second, there is an observable (but not as easily measured) improvement in students' feelings about school. Third, there is a subtle change to a healthier climate throughout the school. And finally, there are signs of a school developing the characteristics that everyone wants for it: independence, cooperation, sharing, and teamwork among students and faculty.

"I would never again try to teach reading without tutors. They give my children the kind of practice and help needed, and they give so much more help than I can. Even a poor tutor can give a young child more assistance than can a teacher working with a whole class."

       First Grade Teacher
       Pacoima Elementary School

"This school is different than it used to be. We talk about truly important things, we interact more with each other, we do things differently, and we've begun to improve. The whole atmosphere in the school is changing for the better."

       Resource Teacher
       Pacoima Elementary School

PHILOSOPHY OF INTERGRADE TUTORING

Underlying all the activities, procedures, and materials that compose the intergrade tutoring program described in this manual is a viewpoint regarding education shaped along these lines:

- Students *can* learn. Children want to learn, if only because they are innately curious. A failure to learn results from a failure to teach. When a student does not learn, it is not because of who he is, or his background, or his family, or his environment. It is, simply, a matter of ineffective instruction.

- To be effective, instruction must be tailored to the individual needs of students. Every student is unique, and his instruction must address that individuality. This is difficult in a setting with large numbers of students of wide-ranging abilities. It is even more difficult in an underachieving school because of the school's history of failure, the urgent need for students to catch up, and the widened range of achievement levels that underachievement brings.

- One powerful tool for carrying out individualized instruction is intergrade tutoring. Its basic features are:
  1. Goals are established for tutoring.
  2. Tutoring materials and procedures are developed.
  3. Students are trained in tutoring skills.
  4. Tutors work one-to-one with learners.

5. The teacher plays an integral part in the tutoring system.
6. The program is monitored, evaluated, and modified.

- New roles and relationships will develop in an intergrade tutoring school. Simply rubbing an older child against a younger one does not necessarily ignite the spark of learning. Teachers must actively participate in the tutoring process to make sure it works. A new role is therefore created for the teacher: manager of an instructional system. The principal also assumes a new role: leader in the change process, supporter of growth and development. A new position is created: coordinator of tutoring. And parents hold a new lease on their children's education: as participants in the process of change and growth.

HOW ABOUT *PEER* TUTORING?

Many people in schools are interested in *peer* tutoring—having students in a given class, all approximately the same age, tutor one another. The basic principles of intergrade tutoring are applicable to a situation in which peers tutor each other. Teachers who have experienced the Workshop on Tutoring described in this book have successfully carried over the procedures to peer tutoring within their own classrooms, even though the Tutorial Community Program—and thus this manual, which describes the TCP model—happened to be based upon the intergrade tutoring approach.

Most teachers use peer tutoring naturally, although they may not think of it as "tutoring." It is common for teachers to ask one student to work with another, or to direct a student with a problem to a classmate for assistance. These casual approaches certainly are useful, but teachers using systematic intergrade tutoring have discovered greater benefits when peer tutoring is based on principles and procedures from the intergrade model.

Throughout this book adjustments necessary for using the intergrade tutorial model for peer tutoring purposes are indicated. Unless specified to the contrary, any statement in this manual is intended to apply to peer tutoring as well as to intergrade tutoring.

". . . the failure-to-learn characteristic of low-income, minority-group pupils is due more to deficiencies in the schools themselves than to deficiencies in the pupil or his environment. . . the mission of the schools is to teach children no matter what their state of readiness. When traditional or conventional practices do not succeed, the school is responsible for finding other means of teaching effectively and, if necessary, for changing its concepts and methods drastically in order to do so."

Gerald Weinstein and Mario Fantini
Toward Humanistic Education

"I had my doubts about tutoring when it was started. Then I visited a lot of classrooms, and saw for myself the results. Now my concern is with how we can help the tutoring program to grow."

Member of a Parents' Advisory Council

OVERVIEW: INITIATING INTERGRADE TUTORING

Succeeding sections of this document contain the information a school-community needs to put into practice an intergrade tutoring program composed of four phases.*

Phase	Basic Ingredients	Approximate Time Required
I. Exploration	School and community decide to adopt an intergrade tutoring program. Tutoring Coordinator is appointed.	1 month
II. Planning	Plans are made for intergrade tutoring: instructional area, objectives, evaluation procedures, tutoring procedures.	1 month
III. Preparation	Teachers are prepared for intergrade tutoring, and older students are trained as tutors.	2 months
IV. Implementation	Tutoring process is carried out. Actual tutoring is done for a period of time, is evaluated, necessary revisions are made, and tutoring recommences.	6 months

The rest of this document is divided into two sections:

1. "Making Intergrade Tutoring Work," which contains descriptions of the steps involved in the four phases. This section is written for everyone concerned with the school: administrators, teachers, and parents.

2. "The Tutoring Process: Some Details," in which essential aspects of each step in the sequence are developed. This section is written primarily for the two key people who have major responsibilities for leading the development of the program: the principal and the tutoring coordinator.

"... one realizes that the idea of each teaching another may indeed be a revolutionary step toward maintaining community in a society where the forces of urban organization, of mass production, and indeed of mass education are all centrifugal."

Jerome Bruner
"Toward a Sense of Community"

---

*If the reader is interested in peer tutoring rather than intergrade tutoring, certain aspects of the four phases will not apply; these will be pointed out where appropriate.

Making Intergrade Tutoring Work

An Overview

Effective tutoring does not just happen. To really work—to reach the goals hoped for from it—a tutoring program must be planned, implemented, monitored, and modified systematically.

This section treats the design of a systematic tutoring program. The design is made up of four phases: Exploration, Planning, Preparation, and Implementation. For each phase there is a "flow chart" of activities and a treatment of the steps involved.

A note of caution: This design evolved over a period of time, after considerable trial-and-error, and has proved to be workable. A school should protect itself from repeating unnecessary mistakes. Care should be used before major changes are made to this design.

And a note of hope: While the design may seem elaborate, the ideas contained within it are simple. Approach the design with confidence and a relaxed attitude, and it will prove to be manageable. Carry it out and the results will be rewarding.

This section provides only a brief overview of the steps in the design of intergrade tutoring. Ample details can be found in the section, "The Tutoring Process: Some Details." Cross-references are provided. A flowchart of the steps is on the following two pages.

Sequence of Activities for Intergrade Tutoring

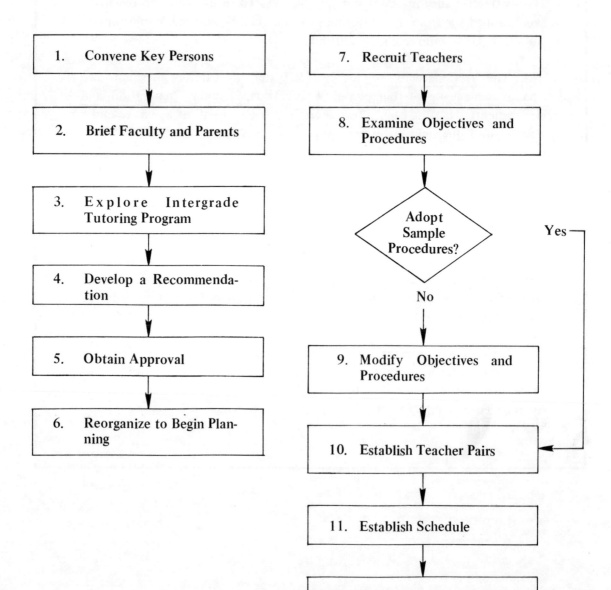

EXPLORATION PHASE: 1 MONTH   **PLANNING PHASE: 1 MONTH**

1. Convene Key Persons

2. Brief Faculty and Parents

3. Explore Intergrade Tutoring Program

4. Develop a Recommendation

5. Obtain Approval

6. Reorganize to Begin Planning

7. Recruit Teachers

8. Examine Objectives and Procedures

Adopt Sample Procedures?   Yes

No

9. Modify Objectives and Procedures

10. Establish Teacher Pairs

11. Establish Schedule

12. Notify Parents

Sequence of Activities for Intergrade Tutoring
(continued)

PREPARATION PHASE: 2 MONTHS   IMPLEMENTATION PHASE: 6 MONTHS

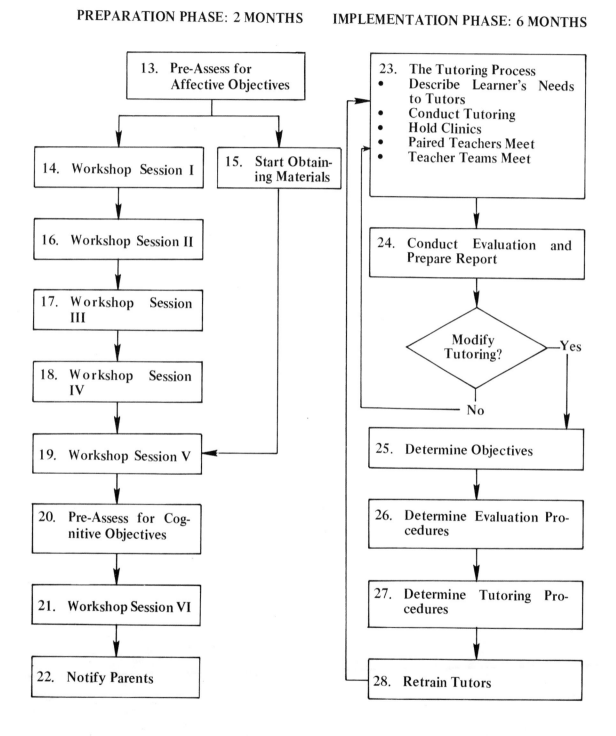

13. Pre-Assess for Affective Objectives

14. Workshop Session I

15. Start Obtaining Materials

16. Workshop Session II

17. Workshop Session III

18. Workshop Session IV

19. Workshop Session V

20. Pre-Assess for Cognitive Objectives

21. Workshop Session VI

22. Notify Parents

23. The Tutoring Process
- Describe Learner's Needs to Tutors
- Conduct Tutoring
- Hold Clinics
- Paired Teachers Meet
- Teacher Teams Meet

24. Conduct Evaluation and Prepare Report

Modify Tutoring?   Yes   No

25. Determine Objectives

26. Determine Evaluation Procedures

27. Determine Tutoring Procedures

28. Retrain Tutors

Phase I: Exploration

"We have increasing and persuasive evidence to the effect that large segments of the public are dissatisfied with the performance of our educational system. And, as a nation propelled by a tradition of educational idealism, and relatively unencumbered by material scarcity, we are under a strong compulsion to fulfill the goals (for education); our national conscience will be haunted by anything less than perfection of our educational system."

James Guthrie and Edward Wynne
New Models for American Education

Why does a school institute a tutoring program? Generally such a decision grows out of an awareness at a school that changes are needed to improve the education of the children. Maybe the answer lies in a tutoring program. Maybe it does not. Before plunging into a new mode of operation, a school must carefully determine its needs and capabilities. Is change indeed needed? If an intergrade tutoring program is the answer, how should it be implemented? How can the school be most effectively organized to transition itself toward a mode of shared responsibility and mutual support?

What kind of school might embark on a tutoring program? A school that admits that children are not achieving all they should in one or more areas. A school that recognizes that teachers need to develop better instructional procedures. A school that accepts responsibility for doing whatever is necessary to give its students the education they deserve.

Once a school has probed the merits of a tutoring program and found them valid, it should embark on the program in careful stages.

Some schools may wish to have a few teachers try out the program on a pilot basis before adopting it school-wide. This approach should be handled with great tact to avoid the impression of favoritism for a chosen few. Even if only several teachers participate in the initial tutoring, the entire staff should be involved with the planning, preparation, implementation, and evaluation, and a date should be set when all will engage in the tutoring project. An alternative approach is that everyone begins together with a minimal program, which is then gradually expanded. The judgment on which approach is more successful awaits further experience.

To make the program truly effective, and incidentally provide a model of cooperation for the students, a partnership of administration, teachers, and parents must be established early. Developing an organization that thrives on shared decision-making and mutual support is a major task that calls for changes in traditional ways of operating and lines of communication. Key personnel, especially the principal, must provide the leadership to try out the various processes involved in the tutoring program. A Tutoring Coordinator must provide the daily assistance to assure successful implementation of each step in the process. Spurred by their example, the rest of the school-community contributes to building an effective program.

"The real reason should be to get us an inch on the way toward making the helper and the helped the universal unit of exchange with a culture that continues to produce lonely crowds, lonelier than ever."

Jerome Bruner
"Toward a Sense of Community"

"It is time for us to recognize that successful efforts at planned change must take as a primary target the improvement of organizational health—the school system's ability not only to function effectively, but to develop and grow to a more fully functioning system."

Matthew Miles
Change Process in the Public Schools

The sequence of activities in how a school might typically explore a tutoring program, leading to an intelligent recommendation and decision, is briefly summarized below.*

1. **CONVENE KEY PERSONS.** The principal holds meetings with key personnel of the school (parents' advisory council chairmen, faculty chairmen) to discuss the need for educational improvement, consider the intergrade tutoring program, and decide whether to involve the total staff and parents in further exploration. If the key personnel decide that change is needed and that the program has promise, they establish a task force to work with the principal and to coordinate the decision-making process. Continuing involvement, guidance, and support from the key persons is essential to the success of a program.

2. **BRIEF FACULTY AND PARENTS.** The information developed by the key persons is now shared with the faculty and parents (usually the advisory council) by the principal. They are given an overview of the intergrade tutoring program, and are asked for reactions. They should be told that all aspects of the program will be thoroughly explored before any decision is made.

3. **EXPLORE INTERGRADE TUTORING PROGRAM.** This step involves a careful study of what is involved in implementing an intergrade tutoring program. The task force studies the descriptions of Phases II, III, and IV of the tutoring program in this manual, visits other involved schools, and thoroughly discusses the underlying assumptions and basic concepts. The requirements for personnel, responsibilities, materials, organization, staff development, facilities, and schedule changes are carefully explored. Through this exploration, the task force will become familiar with the sequence of activities to plan, prepare, and implement the program.

4. **DEVELOP A RECOMMENDATION.** Now the task force is ready to develop an overall design of an intergrade tutoring program for the school. The sample design as outlined in Phases II, III, and IV of this manual should be followed as closely as possible and

---

*Readers choosing to use peer tutoring instead of intergrade tutoring should substitute that phrase in place of "intergrade tutoring" in these six steps, and in subsequent steps described below.

amended only with great care. The group's recommendation will include: number of teachers to be involved (everyone or a few to continue the exploration?); number of classes; a schedule for the planning, preparation and implementation phases; personnel and responsibilities (including a full-time Tutoring Coordinator and other helping personnel to provide ongoing program support); and considerations for budget, materials, and facilities. The specific planning for tutoring procedures is not done at this time; it will take place during the planning phase if the program is accepted.

5. **OBTAIN APPROVAL.** The final recommendation is presented to the principal and then by him to the faculty and community for approval and support. Enough time provided for thorough understanding at this point will pay off in the future by avoiding differing perceptions of the purposes and procedures of the program.

6. **REORGANIZE TO BEGIN PLANNING.** If the program is approved, a Tutoring Coordinator and other support personnel are appointed and responsibilities are assigned.

The Tutoring Coordinator is the staff person to work out details so that the administration and the staff have the information they need to make decisions. He or she will be responsible for working with committees to determine tutoring objectives and procedures, developing the details for schedules and use of facilities, and for coordinating the preparation of materials. He will be responsible for conducting the workshops for teachers, overseeing implementation, and working with any additional helping personnel in providing ongoing support and evaluation. He will document the results for presentation to the principal, faculty, and parent advisory council.

The selection of the Tutoring Coordinator is a vital step in a successful program. The task force should review the "Note to the Tutoring Coordinator" which appears on page 41, develop a job description, advertise for interested teachers to apply, and select the Coordinator based on their estimate of the person's ability to meet the needs of the position. The task force should realize, however, that this is a unique position and teachers normally are not required to possess the skills called for.

As soon as this organization is established, the school is ready to begin the planning phase.

"Educators must live with the stark reality that there is no short cut to rational decision making. The process is often tedious and painstaking. Rational decision making comes only from a vigorous give-and-take in a colloquy, the means by which professionals have always resolved conflicts and come to ultimate decisions."

Donald Myers
Decision Making in Curriculum
and Instruction

Phase II: Planning

In this phase the planning of the intergrade tutoring program is carried out. When this phase is completed, the groundwork for an effective program will have been laid. The goal of this phase is the completion of the necessary advance work so that participants are clear about what will happen, how, and when, and can tackle their assignments with confidence and enthusiasm.

"For too many years educators have been concerned with what happens to the teacher, not with what happens to the learner. The time for that misdirected concern is over. The sensible conception of instruction is a goal-referenced model. We must set out systematically to improve the degree to which teachers can attain prespecified objectives with learners."

> *James Popham and Eva Baker*
> **Systematic Instruction**

"Planned change demands inputs from numerous sources so that wise decisions can be made; in a school this means the contributions from all members of the staff should be included in planning. Where the staff is united for the achievement of mutually derived goals—where there is an atmosphere of cooperation—planned change can occur."

> *Jerrold Novotney*
> **The Principal and the Challenge**
> **of Change**

---

7. **RECRUIT TEACHERS.** If the task force has decided to initiate intergrade tutoring with only teachers who are definitely interested, those teachers must be recruited. The Tutoring Coordinator and the principal contact teachers they feel might be interested and discuss with them the concept of intergrade tutoring. Efforts should be made to recruit those teachers who will be most likely to devote the necessary time and effort to make the first tutoring efforts successful. If the task force does not limit involvement to volunteers, the entire staff should be informed in detail of their forthcoming participation in the program. In particular, teachers should have all their questions answered and any misunderstandings clarified.

8. **EXAMINE OBJECTIVES AND PROCEDURES.** Teachers who have elected to implement tutoring, along with the Tutoring Coordinator and the principal, study the sample objectives and tutoring procedures described in "The Tutoring Process: Some Details" (page 123). The group determines whether or not to use the sample procedures for the first tutoring cycle. (If the group chooses to use the sample procedures, omit Step 9.)

9. **MODIFY OBJECTIVES AND PROCEDURES.** If a group has decided that the sample procedures are inappropriate, they may modify them or develop their own. Such

would be the case if a group chose to initiate tutoring in a different academic area (e.g., mathematics, social studies) or chose to focus on reading objectives, other than the three in the sample procedures. Some guidelines for preparing tutoring procedures are described in "The Tutoring Process: Some Details" (pages 46-49).

10. **ESTABLISH TEACHER PAIRS.*** The Tutoring Coordinator and the principal now pair upper grade and lower grade teachers for tutoring. Teacher pairing is not to be treated lightly. A tutoring program may swim or sink on the basis of the way tutoring partners are selected. Two don'ts: don't select pairs at random, nor on the basis of personal friendship. The basic do: do form pairs on the basis of compatibility in teachers' classroom behavior. Teacher requests should not be ignored, but pairings still should be based on the above criteria.

11. **ESTABLISH SCHEDULE.** Scheduling means establishing a master calendar by answering questions concerning the preparation phase, the tutoring period, and the time between tutoring cycles. The schedule is prepared by the Tutoring Coordinator and principal with input from teachers; it is published and distributed to all persons involved with the program.

12. **NOTIFY PARENTS.** It's now time to notify parents about the intergrade tutoring program. Soon their children will be involved in pretutoring activities, and parents should not be surprised by this. Meetings are held with existing parent groups where the program is described and questions answered. Letters are sent home to all parents of participating children, briefly describing the program and their children's participation in it.

"Once an instructor decides he will teach his students something, several kinds of activities are necessary on his part if he is to succeed. He must first decide upon the goals he intends to reach at the end of his course or program. He must then select procedures, content, and methods that are relevant to the objectives; cause the students to interact with appropriate subject matter in accordance with principles of learning; and, finally, measure or evaluate the student's performance according to the objectives or goals originally selected."

Robert Mager
Preparing Instructional Objectives

---

*This step does not apply to peer tutoring.

Phase III: Preparation

In this phase, preparations are made for the initiation of intergrade tutoring. When this phase is completed, teachers are prepared, tutors are trained, and all materials are available. Tutoring is ready to start.*

"The Workshop on Tutoring was really good. It was very helpful to a teacher new to tutoring, especially because I was aware of the next steps."

> *Third Grade Teacher*
> *Norwood Elementary School*

"Having a complete tutoring plan was a great help. It gave me something concrete to start with. We found lots of ways to extend the plan and do even more things with the kids."

> *Sixth Grade Teacher*
> *Plainview Elementary School*

Note: As mentioned above, the details for most of the following steps are found in "The Tutoring Process: Some Details" beginning on page 39.

13. **PRE-ASSESS FOR AFFECTIVE OBJECTIVES**. Earlier, objectives were defined, and now evaluation procedures are put into use. Students are measured on affective objectives to obtain baseline data for later comparison with data collected after the tutoring cycle. Affective objectives should be pre-assessed now, since students will soon be involved in pre-tutoring activities which will already begin to affect their attitudes toward school. The identical evaluation procedures should be used both before and after the tutoring cycle.

14. **WORKSHOP SESSION I.** This session, titled "Getting Ready," focuses on the importance of planning. Paired teachers practice planning their tutoring program. Between this session and the next one paired teachers draw up their initial plans.

15. **START OBTAINING MATERIALS.** While the workshop is going on, the materials needed for tutoring are assembled. Some materials will already be in the school and only need to be collected. Others may have to be purchased. And many support materials (such as record-keeping forms) will be produced by the school. All this takes time, and work should begin early. Tutoring materials must be ready by Workshop Session V for use in the training of tutors and the preparation of teachers.

16. **WORKSHOP SESSION II.** Titled "Getting Acquainted," Session II treats the development of friendly relationships between the students in paired classes. Two ways of

---

*Readers implementing peer tutoring will recognize the need to modify some portions of the Workshop on Tutoring described here. In the first session teachers develop plans on an individual basis rather than as pairs. The socialization activity in session two does not apply. And in the third session the observation activity is not necessary.

developing good relations are covered: informal get-togethers for the two classes and an interview project for the students. Between sessions, teachers conduct an informal "socialization" and the interview project.

17. **WORKSHOP SESSION III**. In this session, "More About Younger Students," teachers learn about having tutors observe younger students in the classroom and about a training session for tutors called, "Difficulties Children Have in Learning." Between sessions, the teachers arrange for the observation and conduct the training session on "Difficulties."

18. **WORKSHOP SESSION IV**. During this session, teachers learn about two more training sessions for tutors, "Ways to Help a Younger Student Feel Important and Successful" and "Understanding the Teacher." Then they conduct the two sessions with tutors.

19. **WORKSHOP SESSION V**. In Session V, "Specific Tutoring Procedures," teachers go over the training of tutors in the specific tutoring procedures adopted. Afterwards, they conduct that training with the tutors. A reminder: All tutoring materials must be ready at this point.

20. **PRE-ASSESS FOR COGNITIVE OBJECTIVES**. At this point both tutors and younger students are assessed for the cognitive objectives determined earlier. As was true with step 13 (Pre-Assess for Affective Objectives), the pre-assessment is designed to provide baseline data for later comparison with data collected at the end of the tutoring cycle. The assessment tests given the students must be identical to those given after the tutoring cycle.

21. **WORKSHOP SESSION VI**. This session, called "Ongoing Support for Tutors," covers the regular meeting between teachers and tutors after tutoring has begun. Teachers learn about observing the tutoring process and about holding "clinics" with tutors. They then demonstrate the clinic to the tutors. This ends the Workshop for teachers and the training of tutors. Tutoring is now ready to begin.

22. **NOTIFY PARENTS**. Once again, parents are informed about tutoring. This time, they are told that the preparations are completed and that tutoring will start on a certain day and go on for a specified time period.

"If one learns how to learn, one can be a learner in a great number of areas. A child, in order to teach another child material, needs to learn the material better in the first place; he needs to organize it, needs to observe another learner, and make contact with that learner. In essence, he must become a manager of learning and he may become more aware about learning; all this contributes to learning how to learn."

Alan Gartner, Mary Kohler, Frank Riessman
Children Teach Children

Phase IV: Implementation

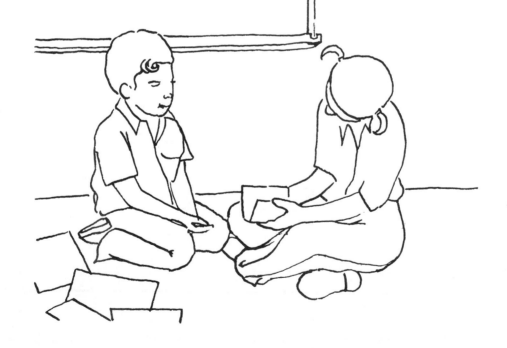

Homework:

Reader pgs. 74-87
Workbook - units 5+6

In the fourth phase, actual tutoring is conducted, evaluated, and modified if needed. This phase culminates the planning and preparation that have preceded it. Now the results of the earlier work are seen.

"One thing I really like about our tutoring program is that my pupils know what they're supposed to do when they tutor. When they come back to our room they're pleased by their success and eager to do their own work."

Fourth Grade Teacher
Plainview Elementary School

"The first time I tried tutoring it was a casual, haphazard arrangement. And it didn't work. The last two years we used a planned tutoring program. My children learned from it, the tutors were happy, and I was able to do so much more with my children and the tutors."

Second Grade Teacher
Pacoima Elementary School

---

23. **THE TUTORING PROCESS.** Step 23 is the heart of the tutoring. It is made up of five elements, all of which contribute to effective intergrade tutoring.

- **Describe Learners' Needs to Tutors.** First, the receiving teacher meets with the tutors and describes the needs of the individual learners with whom they will each be working. The tutors already know something about the students from their earlier socializations, interviews, and observations. What they need now is a detailed statement of the particular learning needs on which to focus when they tutor. For example, if the subject matter is mathematics, a teacher might tell some tutors the following:

  "Jack, you'll be helping Robert. He is having trouble with regrouping when he does subtraction, so be sure you concentrate on regrouping. Martha, Betty needs to work on simple addition, so spend time on adding one-digit numbers. Don, when you help Vic, I want you to give him plenty of practice in place value. He's been having trouble understanding that and keeps making mistakes in both addition and subtraction."

- **Conduct Tutoring.** Now the actual tutoring is conducted. As older and younger children get together, the tutors put into practice what they've learned about tutoring. Teachers participate in the tutoring by moving about the room, helping tutors and learners, suggesting fresh approaches to tutors, observing tutors in action, etc. The major role for the teacher is that of a resource to the students. Possessed of a great deal of expertise that tutors don't have, the teacher uses that expertise to assure that tutoring is successful. As an integral part of the tutoring act, the teacher promotes a spirit of teamwork among the teacher and the tutors.

- **Hold Clinics.** Each week the teachers and tutors meet in what is called a "clinic" during which they discuss their experiences and work out solutions to problems. Teachers discuss their observations of the tutors and give them any required training or retraining. Tutors describe their experiences and draw upon each other and the teachers for help in overcoming problems. These meetings are important for the further development of tutors' skills. They're also critical for providing tutors with support and feedback: an upper grade student needs to hear from teachers that he is doing well, that he is really helping the child he works with, and that he can overcome any obstacles to success that he has encountered.

- **Paired Teachers Meet.** The two paired teachers meet weekly to review their program and plan its future. No matter how well the program was planned originally, there are bound to be things that were overlooked or treated too lightly in the original plans. These oversights surface as the tutoring goes on. Original plans must be reworked; new plans must be made. The paired teachers should view their program as unfinished and flexible as they meet together regularly to see what needs to be modified and how.

- **Teacher Teams Meet.** Finally, teacher teams meet to give one another ideas, support, and feedback. Just as tutors ask each other for help, teachers involved in tutoring pose problems and ask their peers to help solve them. A teacher asking for help will find that the problem is not news to the rest. Most likely, others have experienced the same problem and have found ways to deal with it. Besides serving as a forum for discussing common problems, the teacher team meetings also raise confidence and boost morale as teachers see they are all working together.

"... the role of the teacher is to support growth rather than maintain control. You become a promotor of collaboration, and establisher of the norms of helpfulness rather than competition. You delegate responsibility and share the limelight. In turn, you get a high level of cooperation and commitment to learning. The youngsters enjoy school more because they are more successful. The olders grow in academic achievement, gain insights, and learn service-oriented techniques."

Peggy Lippitt
"Children Can Teach Other Children"

"A frequently repeated theme indicated that good ideas came from other teachers. This may suggest the importance of the team concept which has not yet been fully developed in the elementary school."

Institute for the Development of
Educational Activities
A Symposium on the Training of
Teachers: Elementary School

---

24. **CONDUCT EVALUATION AND PREPARE REPORT**. After a prespecified time period, the tutoring cycle is completed and a total evaluation is conducted. Cognitive and affective objectives for tutors and learners are assessed through the tests, questionnaires, and observation techniques designed earlier. Staff and parent reactions to tutoring are obtained through questionnaires. The data are collected and summarized in a report that describes and interprets the results.

This evaluation is intended to answer certain basic questions: Has our tutoring program met its objectives? If not, how should it be modified? What additional objectives should be incorporated?

A detailed written report is presented to the staff and school-related parent groups. If possible, it should be accompanied by an oral presentation. A briefer report is sent to all parents.

25. **MODIFY TUTORING?** On the basis of the report and discussions of it among staff members and parent groups, the school staff decides whether or not to modify the tutoring program. If the program is deemed successful and not in need of modification, the tutoring process will recommence for another cycle. In such a case, it is wise to consider how soon to begin again (immediately or after a short respite) and how long a time period to conduct tutoring (same as before, shorter, or longer).

Chances are that the program will require some modification, perhaps to address a new instructional area or sub-area. If so, the staff repeats the previous cycle. Thus, in **step 25**, new objectives are determined; in **step 26**, evaluation procedures are determined; in **step 27**, new tutoring procedures are determined; and in **step 28**, additional training for the new procedures is given to tutors. The tutoring then begins anew.

The Tutoring Process:
Some Details

You will be playing an extremely important role in successfully implementing intergrade tutoring in your school. So that you can be prepared to play that role, this Note summarizes some activities tutoring coordinators previously have discovered to be essential.

- **Planning Phase**

    Study This Manual. Become familiar with its content. Especially, look in depth at the Sample Tutoring Procedures (p. 123) and the Workshop on Tutoring (p. 57).

    Contact Teachers. Along with the principal, make individual contacts with teachers about tutoring. Discover the most promising candidates to initiate tutoring in your school.

    Lead Planning Meetings. Be responsible for leading meetings of teachers as they examine the Sample Tutoring Procedures and plan subsequent actions. Schedule the meetings, plan the agendas, and lead the group to make decisions.

    Plan Teacher Pairs. Do the advance thinking about which teachers should be paired for tutoring. Make recommendations about pairings to your principal and to the teachers.

    Plan the Master Schedule. Think ahead about the schedule of events in carrying out tutoring. Recommend a master schedule to your principal and to your teachers.

    Prepare Parents' Letter. Assure that the letter notifying parents of the tutoring program is written and that sufficient copies are reproduced.

- **Preparation Phase**

    Oversee Pretesting. Make certain that materials are ready for the pre-assessment of students. Help teachers conduct the assessment.

    Get Materials Ready. Take steps needed to be sure tutoring materials are ready for use at the time of Workshop Session V.

    Lead the Workshop. Conduct the Workshop on Tutoring. Help teachers with the tasks called for during the Workshop.

- **Implementation Phase**

Check on Progress. Find ways to keep yourself informed on the progress teachers are making.

Encourage People. Students, teachers, and parents will need encouragement as difficulties arise. You will need to find ways to support them when they grapple with problems.

Be There. When important things happen, you should be there—to be informed, to help out, and to spread the word about it.

Escort Visitors. Tutoring schools receive visitors. You should be available to escort visitors and discuss your school's tutoring program.

Promote Tutoring. Take the initiative for promoting the concept of tutoring within your school. Talk about the program and its accomplishments with non-involved teachers, parents, etc.

Think Ahead. Do the advance planning so that you and your school will be prepared for critical steps when their time comes (end-of-cycle evaluations, planning for next year, etc.).

Help Train Tutors. Some teachers may need assistance with their tutor training. Along the way a few tutors may need some additional personal help. You can give this kind of training.

Help Dissolve Concerns. Be available and helpful in dealing with concerns of students, teachers, or parents.

Observe and Give Feedback. Drop by and observe the various dimensions of the program: tutor training sessions, clinics, paired teacher meetings, actual tutoring. Afterwards, give the participants honest feedback on your observations.

Encourage Sharing. See to it that the good ideas, procedures, and materials are shared among all participants. Use group meetings to promote sharing.

Release Teachers. One important way teachers learn new techniques is through observing each other. Help free up teachers so they have opportunities to see what others are doing.

Clerical Tasks. Many seemingly minor clerical tasks can strengthen the program. Assume responsibility for tasks like preparing materials, producing a "newsletter" of anecdotes and ideas, obtaining badges for tutors, writing reports, etc.

Develop Materials. As tutoring progresses there may be need for additional tutoring materials. Work with teachers to develop and/or revise such materials.

Pick up Slack. Sometimes the program bogs down as one member of the team can't fulfill a responsibility. Look out for such occurrences and move in to fill the gap.

Learn About Tutoring. Try to broaden your own knowledge concerning tutoring. Talk with others, visit other schools, read about tutoring—and bring new ideas, literature, and materials to your school.

Help Solve Problems. Don't let problems remain unsolved. Don't assume they will work themselves out or that nothing can be done. Help teachers work through problems to acceptable solutions.

ESTABLISHING TEACHER PAIRS*

The Tutoring Coordinator and principal have the responsibility for pairing upper grade and lower grade teachers for tutoring. These two teachers, and the students in their classes, are going to work close together for quite a while, so their pairing is not a casual matter. If the pairing is done randomly, or by putting together personal friends, the results will be unproductive if the much-needed similarity in philosophy and approach to students is missing.

The probability of strong pairs resulting is increased if the principal and Coordinator consider the five dimensions listed below and look for the greatest degree of compatibility between upper grade and lower grade teachers.

1. **Classroom Atmosphere.** Does the teacher maintain a formal atmosphere or a more informal one?

2. **Daily Schedule.**, Does the teacher follow a carefully planned schedule or have a flexible one that responds to student interests?

3. **Types of Lessons.** Does the teacher typically work with students in large groups or maintain an individualized approach with little group work?

4. **Student Misbehavior.** Does the teacher have very low tolerance for misbehavior or is some misbehavior acceptable?

5. **Classroom Standards.** Are standards for the class known to all and carefully observed or does the teacher view standards as unimportant?

When paired teachers are not compatible along most of these dimensions, the result is disharmony between them and frustration for the tutors who shuttle back and forth between two opposing environments. The Coordinator and principal must make sure that the pairs, and their students, find the two situations very similar.

ESTABLISHING A SCHEDULE

A number of events will take place in the weeks after the planning phase is complete. The principal and Coordinator have to make decisions related to these events and establish a master calendar of time periods required. This means answering these questions:

1. When will the preparation phase be carried out? When will workshop sessions begin and end? On what day of the week and at what time will the workshop be held?

2. How long will tutoring go on? Tutoring should not be an indefinite process that rolls on as long as interest lasts and results are positive. Instead, it should be planned for a specific time period: six weeks, eight weeks, ten weeks.

3. How long a time period will there be between tutoring cycles? How long should be allocated for the program evaluation period? How long for the next planning period?

In answering these questions, a calendar for 40 weeks in a school year is used (see page 51). After holidays, vacations, and special occurrences are filled in, the questions above are answered to fit in best with the calendar. This planning avoids some disastrous pitfalls, such

---

*This discussion does not apply to schools implementing peer tutoring.

as ending a tutoring cycle right before a lengthy vacation, resulting in a delayed and therefore less reliable evaluation.

Once the calendar is completed, it is published and distributed to all parties concerned, and discussed at a faculty meeting and a meeting of the parents' group. A sample calendar appears at the end of this section.

PREPARING TUTORING PROCEDURES

To be effective, tutors must be trained in specific procedures to follow when they work with a younger student. When tutors are not equipped with carefully planned procedures, their self-developed efforts often fail and they experience frustration and defeat. Although the specific tutoring procedures will vary from one subject to another, they should be based on the following general principles.

• **Tutors must provide opportunities for learners to practice what they are supposed to learn.** The objectives and the related evaluation procedures will indicate the type of behavior the learner is to evidence when he has mastered the objective. For example, if an objective is to master sight vocabulary words, young learners must practice saying words when the words are shown to them. One way is through reading text material. Another way is through flashcard drill on the words to be learned. Tutoring procedures that incorporate both of these activities provide learners with appropriate practice for the behavior they are to learn.

If mastery of addition with regrouping is an objective, learners should practice the steps involved in regrouping numbers and adding them. This can be done by using pages in a mathematics workbook containing problems in addition with regrouping. It also can be done by preparing special worksheets of addition problems requiring regrouping. Either or both of these tasks built into the tutoring procedures give learners practice appropriate to their objective.

• **Practice must be frequent.** Young students must be given as many practice trials as needed to master a given objective. "As needed" is the key phrase: some young learners master an objective quickly after only a few practice trials; others require larger numbers of practice trials. The tutoring procedures should take this into account and provide means by which a tutor can give his learner the number of trials the younger student needs.

One obvious conclusion is that the reliance on consumable instructional materials does not answer the needs of all students. Having learners complete pages in a workbook gives each one a fixed number of practice trials, sufficient for some but inadequate for others. And since the page has been done—written upon—it cannot be used again. One answer is to provide plastic overlays on which learners write with crayons, so that a page can be re-used if needed. A second answer is to develop additional examples of the problems on the workbook page which a tutor uses if his learner needs more practice on a skill.

• **The learner must get knowledge of results.** Long practice by itself is useless unless the learner knows whether he is getting it right. Tutors must be shown ways of informing the learner that correct responses *are* correct, or how to convey the correct response if the learner is in error.

As part of the knowledge of results, tutors and learners must be aware of their progress toward objectives. This is not so much a procedure for the tutors as it is for the receiving teachers who work with the tutor and learners. As a first step, the teacher determines the interim milestones toward a final objective. For example, when working on sight vocabulary

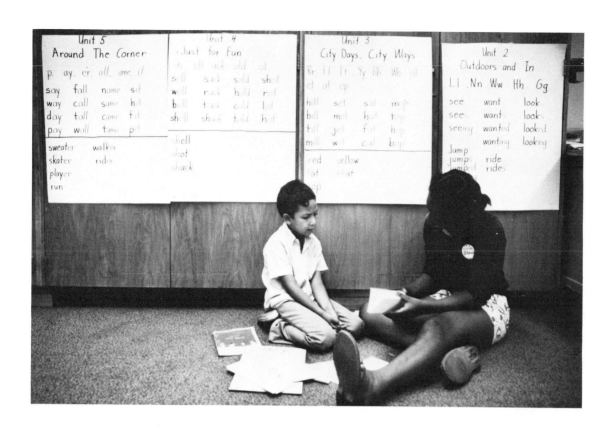

in basal reading texts, the list of vocabulary words can be divided into units and learners assessed on mastery of words within a unit. When a unit has been mastered, teachers inform learners and tutors, letting them know that they are indeed making progress. Similarly, when working on addition the field can be divided into units like one-place addition, two-place addition without regrouping, two-place addition with regrouping. As a learner masters a unit, the teacher lets the two students know that that much progress has occurred.

• **Tutoring procedures must include record-keeping**, so that learners, tutors, and teachers have permanent records of what was done, when, and how well. Two types of records are called for: one kept by tutors to record daily activities; another kept by teachers to keep track of progress through the interim units described above.

Records kept by tutors need to be simple. Extensive writing discourages them. One method is to give each tutor a "log" in the form of a calendar, on which the tutor notes the things done each day (pages read in a book, workbook pages completed, special worksheets completed), and how well the tutoring session went (very good, ok, not good).

Teachers' record-keeping forms should also be simple. (Extensive writing will discourage anyone!) If the forms are too elaborate, they will gather dust. One simple procedure is to draw a table on which the units in sequence are shown in columns at the top, with rows for the names of the learners. As a learner masters a unit, the teacher marks it off on the table with a check, a star, or by coloring in the square.

Another useful form is for recording the teacher's observations of how well a tutor performs his tutoring role. A series of questions are posed ("Does the tutor maintain a friendly relationship?," "Does the tutor follow the tutoring procedures correctly?") which are answered by a "yes" or "no." Teachers observe tutors frequently, note how well each tutor did, and discuss the results with tutors. (A sample Tutor Observation Form is given to teachers as part of the Workshop on Tutoring.)

NOTIFYING PARENTS

On three separate occasions, parents are informed about the tutoring program. The first time comes at the end of the planning phase, when the plans are described to the parents' group and a letter is sent by the principal to each parent indicating that a tutoring program will be initiated in the school. The second message comes at the end of the preparation phase, when a letter is sent by teachers to each parent indicating that preparations have been completed and the tutoring process will begin. The third time comes at the end of a tutoring period, when the results of the tutoring are presented to the parents' group. Samples of the first two letters to be sent to all parents are at the end of this section, pages 53 and 55.*

When meetings are held with the parents' group, the Tutoring Coordinator gives the parents as much information as possible and asks for their reactions and suggestions. These meetings have two purposes: providing parents with information on the school's programs so that parents are better informed about what is happening in their school; and giving parents the opportunity to suggest things that might bolster the program. Parental support is vital in any new effort, and knowing that parents approve of a new program can strengthen the faculty's commitment. In addition, parents can help solve problems, for instance, by volunteering to assist in the production and assembly of materials needed for tutoring.

*Both sample letters to parents will require some modification for a peer-tutoring situation.

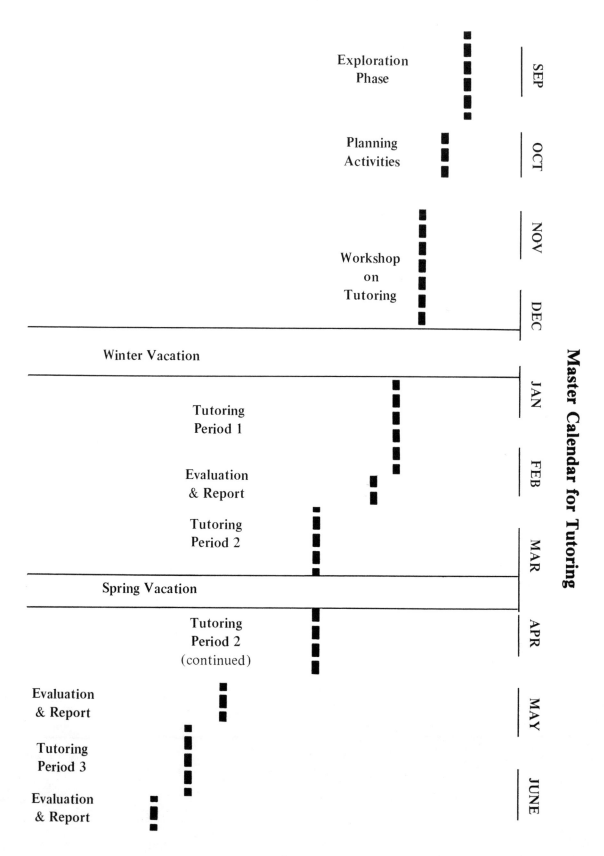

Master Calendar for Tutoring

SEP — Exploration Phase

OCT — Planning Activities

NOV — Workshop on Tutoring

DEC

Winter Vacation

JAN — Tutoring Period 1

FEB — Evaluation & Report

Tutoring Period 2

MAR

Spring Vacation

APR — Tutoring Period 2 (continued)

MAY — Evaluation & Report

Tutoring Period 3

JUNE — Evaluation & Report

51

Sample Principal's Letter to Parents

Date

Dear Parents:

As you may have already heard, our school is initiating a tutoring program in reading. The plans have been developed by the staff over the last several months and reviewed by the Advisory Council at a recent meeting. Upper grade students will be given the opportunity of helping children in younger grades. This will be a regular part of both the older and younger children's school work. It will give upper graders the chance to improve in the reading skills they are helping the younger children master. At the same time, the younger children will get more of the individual attention that every learner needs.

Beginning this week, teachers will be attending workshops, and older and younger children will be involved in activities to prepare them for success in the program. They will get to know each other and establish the friendly relations that are the basis of a good working partnership. Older children will receive special training in how to deal successfully with younger children and how to help them learn to read. They will become trusted members of a team of classmates and teachers who are working on ways to help children learn. Younger children will benefit from the special learning experience and from working with an older child who takes a personal interest in them.

Your child's class will be working with the class of (*paired teacher*). Both teachers will be supervising the tutoring and will be actively involved with the program. Tutoring will begin in about six weeks.

The staff and the students are enthusiastic as we start this new program. If you have any questions, please feel free to call me. The teachers will notify you when the tutoring actually begins.

Sincerely,

Principal

Sample Teachers' Letter to Parents

_____

Date

Dear Parents:

For the past several weeks our classes have been getting ready to begin the tutoring program in reading. Teachers have attended workshops, the children have been getting to know each other as friends, and the older students have been learning how to help a younger child learn to read.

Now we are ready to begin. Next week the tutoring actually starts. The time for tutoring will be each day from _____ to _____. The first session of tutoring in reading will end _____. At that time we will evaluate the success of the program, make any revisions or additions that seem appropriate, and begin another tutoring session.

We encourage you to visit the classes to observe the tutoring in action. Talk to your child about his experience. We would very much like to hear any reactions you have to this new program. If you have any questions, please call or come to see either of us in person.

We are enthusiastic and have high expectations for the success of this tutoring program. We hope you will share our enthusiasm.

Sincerely,

Teacher   Teacher

_(both of the paired teachers
sign letters to both classes)_

A Workshop on Tutoring

This Workshop on Tutoring accomplishes two purposes simultaneously: teachers are prepared for tutoring, and students are trained as tutors. The Workshop consists of six weekly sessions, with follow-on activities for teachers to complete between sessions.

The material which follows is written for the Tutoring Coordinator, who leads the Workshop. The content of each session is described in detail, and handout materials are found at the end of each session's description.

Prior to the Workshop, the Coordinator makes out a large chart (see next page) and displays it at every session. This provides participants with an ongoing overview of the total Workshop.

Occasionally it becomes necessary to build in a "break" in the planned schedule when participants fall behind in completing the tutor training activities (due to illness, unforeseen school events, etc.). The best place for such a "break" is between Sessions IV and V.

A large chart like this should be made out by the Tutoring Coordinator prior to the Workshop and displayed at each Workshop session. Fill in the dates appropriate for your school's Workshop.

Session	Title	Date	Follow-on-Activities
I	Getting Ready		Paired teachers make decisions.
II	Getting Acquainted		Conduct socialization. Conduct interview project.
III	More About Younger Students		Conduct observation. Session on difficulties of younger students.
IV	About Tutoring and Teachers		Session on feeling important and successful. Session on understanding the teacher.
V	Specific Tutoring Procedures		Sessions on specific tutoring procedures.
VI	Ongoing Support for Tutors		Session on the Clinic. Begin tutoring. Observe tutors in action.

Session I. Getting Ready

Background: As the Workshop begins, the school staff has assessed its needs, chosen the instructional area for tutoring, defined the tutoring objectives, and prepared tutoring procedures to reach those objectives. Teacher pairs have been selected.

Purposes of Session: Elicit the teachers' hopes and concerns about the tutoring program.

Provide an exposure to the techniques of (1) leading a discussion and (2) planning.

Initiate the Paired Teacher Planning Meetings.

Agenda:

Topic	Approximate Time	Materials Required
Hopes and Concerns	15-20 minutes	2 large sheets of paper, tape, marking pen
Leading a Discussion	5-10 minutes	"Steps in Leading a Discussion" (TT No. 1)*
Importance of Planning	5-10 minutes	"Teachers' Planning Meeting" (TT No. 2)
Practice: Paired Teacher Planning	20-25 minutes	
Follow On	5-10 minutes	"Teachers' Tutoring Checklist" (TT No. 3)
Evaluation of Session	10-15 minutes	
Total:	60-90 minutes	

*Tutor Training (TT) sheets are included in this manual; see subsequent pages. All TT sheets may be duplicated by the reader for instructional purposes.

HOPES AND CONCERNS (15-20 minutes). What are the teachers' hopes for the tutoring program? Their doubts? Anticipated problems? At the start of Session I, before launching into the details of the tutoring program, give teachers the chance to voice their individual hopes and concerns about tutoring. Then let them briefly discuss these as a group. It breaks the ice, brings out individual and common viewpoints, and helps to set the goals for which you will all strive over the next months.

Take a large sheet of paper and fasten it to the wall. Label it "Hopes." Ask the teachers to think for a minute and to indicate what hopes they have for an intergrade tutoring program. As they name their hopes, avoid discussion. If discussion begins, cut it off gently: there will be time later to discuss things—now we just want to list people's hopes. List each hope on the large sheet of paper; paraphrase and summarize but keep the original meaning. When the naming of hopes has died out, ask them to look at the list of hopes and decide which ones they generally share. Identify the ones shared by most people and mark them.

(After the session, transfer the agreed-upon hopes to another large sheet and display it at each subsequent meeting.)

Take a second large sheet of paper, label it "Concerns," and repeat the activity above. After you have the two lists—Hopes and Concerns—displayed at the front, have the teachers discuss what they can do to achieve their hopes and to alleviate their concerns. They will develop some answers among themselves. But not all items will be answered, especially not all the concerns. They will turn to you for solutions to those concerns ("What *are* we going to do about the work older kids miss?"). You must make it clear that by no means do you have all the answers. In fact, most of the answers lie within them. As the Workshop unfolds, as the tutoring program comes into sharper focus, and—most importantly—as the teachers gain experience, they will develop their own solutions. Emphasize this point. Acceptance of this concept will enable the teachers to step through the tutoring program with confidence.

LEADING A DISCUSSION (5-10 minutes). After hopes and concerns have been discussed, turn the topic to effectively leading a discussion. Indicate that you have been practicing some procedures for leading a discussion during the past minutes. Those procedures will become important for all of them because the tutor training sessions are loaded with discussions. Go over the highlights of the leader's role in leading a discussion. Then give each a copy of "Steps in Leading a Discussion" (Tutor Training No. 1).

IMPORTANCE OF PLANNING (5-10 minutes).* Now turn their attention to the concept of planning. Stress the importance of planning: no effective new program, including tutoring, can be initiated and maintained without adequate planning. "Planning" here means more than just advance planning; it means the continuous shaping and reshaping of plans in the light of ongoing experience.

Basic to this planning process is contact between the paired teachers. The Teachers' Planning Meeting is vital to ultimate success, a point that cannot be stressed enough. Pass out copies of "Teachers' Planning Meeting" (TT No.2) and go over the text at the top. Re-emphasize the necessity for planning. Make sure that everyone understands that Teachers' Planning Meetings are to be held each week.

PRACTICE: PAIRED TEACHER PLANNING (20-25 minutes). Next you will embark

---

*If peer tutoring is being used, the planning activity described here should be carried out by individual teachers. Each teacher should plan tutoring activities among students in the class using the forms "Teachers' Planning Meeting" and "Teachers' Tutoring Checklist" as guides.

on the first of many exercises which lets teachers practice, in the Workshop, the major activities they and their students are expected to perform outside. The first practice session, on planning, is fairly simple and lets the teachers act as themselves. In later practices they will assume other roles, including those of students. These sessions should be live, stimulating, and rewarding.

Tell the group that they will now have a chance to practice holding a planning session. Direct the paired teachers to fan out in twosomes and to take 15 minutes to answer the questions on the lower part of "Teachers' Planning Meeting." Ask them to write down their decisions so that both will have complete records.

As the paired teachers are addressing the questions, circulate and assist any pair that needs help. Some may avoid settling on answers to questions by sliding into other topics. When this happens, bring them back to the task at hand and help them focus on the questions. Be on guard when a pair states they will make their decisions later: few who say so ever do. You will need to exert pressure to get them to make decisions here and now.

At the end of the 15 minutes, call the group together and have each pair report its decisions. Where decisions are lacking, ask other group members to assist that pair ("Can anyone else think of how these two can resolve their dilemma?").

FOLLOW ON (5-10 minutes). Give the group their assignment. Between now and the next session each pair of teachers is to meet and make a number of decisions. Give each a copy of "Teachers' Tutoring Checklist" (TT No. 3) and ask them to meet and answer questions 1 through 12 before the next Workshop session. Note that these decisions are tentative, since later Workshop experiences may cause teachers to revise their decisions; nevertheless, the planning process must begin and the 12 questions need to be answered.

At this point also tell the teachers that Parts B and C of the Teachers' Tutoring Checklist will serve as an ongoing record of their progression through the Workshop. As they complete a module, they will check it off.

EVALUATION OF THE SESSION (10-15 minutes). Tell the group that every Workshop Session will end with a brief evaluation of that session. Throw out two questions: What was good about today's session? and What was wrong with today's session? Make sure their comments are specific ("I liked the way you ran this session." "Can you tell me what particular things I did that you liked?"). Include your own evaluation: how did you feel about yourself as leader, them as participants, and the content of the session? Immediately after the session ends, write down the key comments for future reference.

Steps in Leading a Discussion

1. Arrange the group in a circle or around a table.

2. Have members of the group suggest topics to be covered.
    Write the suggestions on a chalkboard or on a large sheet of paper.

3. Have the group determine priorities: which topics must be taken up today, which can be covered another time.

4. For a given topic, help the group:

    (a) identify clearly the problem/question involved;

    (b) come up with alternative solutions; and

    (c) decide on the most promising alternative.

5. As a leader:

    (a) clarify situations;

    (b) keep the focus on the topic;

    (c) contribute your own ideas;

    (d) ask questions to draw out comments or ideas;

    (e) try to include silent members;

    (f) try to rein in members who monopolize discussions.

6. Reserve time near the end of each meeting to evaluate that meeting for group effectiveness and individual participation.

Teachers' Planning Meeting

A vital part of a successful tutoring program is regular communication between paired teachers. To this end, they will need to provide a period of time on a scheduled basis for planning meetings. Before each meeting, both teachers should write down specific questions to be answered.

Initial meetings will be devoted to planning specific tutoring arrangements and planning for the training of tutors. Key decisions need to be made prior to involving either tutors or learners.

Once tutor training has begun, the teachers' planning meetings will be used to evaluate what has been done and plan for the future. This includes strengthening the successful aspects and planning revisions to less successful parts. These meetings are to be scheduled once a week.

Practice: Teachers' Planning Meeting

> Today you will meet as a pair to answer the questions below. You will have approximately 15 minutes to make these decisions. Then we will come back together to report. Write your decisions in the space provided and keep this sheet.

1. When will we hold our regular weekly planning meetings?
    Day .... Time .... Place ....
2. How many tutors will be involved to start with?
    ....
3. On what basis will the first students be selected to receive help from tutors?
    ....
    On what basis will the first tutors be selected? How will they be paired?
    ....
    Criteria for selecting learners ....
    ....
    Criteria for selecting tutors ....
    ....
    Criteria for pairing tutors and learners ....
    ....

Teachers' Tutoring Checklist

(Check the appropriate item when you have answered the question or completed the task.)

A. Paired teachers meet and make the following decisions:

.... 1. When will ongoing paired teachers' weekly meetings take place?
.... 2. How many students will tutor at the onset?
.... 3. Which students will be involved, as tutors and learners?
.... 4. How will tutors be assigned to learners?
.... 5. When will tutoring take place (time of day, number of days)?
.... 6. Where will tutoring take place?
.... 7. Where will tutoring materials be located?
.... 8. How will both teachers observe tutoring?
.... 9. What will students not involved in tutoring be doing?
..........10. When and where will tutor training take place?
..........11. When will tutoring begin?
..........12. When will ongoing teacher-tutor meetings take place?

B. Orientation training sequence ("sending" teachers' primary responsibility).

.... 1. Tutor-learner socialization.
.... 2. Interview project.
.... 3. Tutors' observation of younger students.
.... 4. Difficulties children have learning.
.... 5. Ways to help younger children.

C. Specific training sequence ("receiving" teacher's primary responsibility).

.... 1. Understanding the teacher's role.
.... 2. Overview of objectives, materials, and procedures.
.... 3. Role-playing each step.
.... 4. Role-playing the tutoring sequence.
.... 5. Clinic as a place to share

- -

The following three ongoing activities are to take place regularly, a minimum of once a week:

1. Paired teachers' meeting
2. Observation of each tutor   } once tutoring begins
3. Teacher-tutor meeting (clinicing)

Session II. Getting Acquainted

Background: At the first session, teachers learned about planning, leading a discussion, and the Paired Teacher Planning Meetings. During the week they were to hold one such meeting and complete questions 1-12 on the Teachers' Tutoring Checklist. Although not specified on the agenda, prior to adjourning Session II you should inquire if anyone had difficulty answering the questions. If so, offer the group's help.

Purposes of Session: Stress importance of building rapport between tutors and learners through (1) socialization and (2) interviews.

Expose teachers to role playing by having them act out the interview project.

Agenda:

Topic	Approximate Time	Materials Required
Establishing Good Rapport	5-10 minutes	
Socialization	5-10 minutes	"Tutor/Learner Socialization" (TT No. 4)
Interview Project	5-10 minutes	"Interview Project" (TT No. 5)
		"Interview Form" (TT No. 6) (at least 3 for all teachers and students in the program)
Role Playing as a Technique	15-20 minutes	"Steps in Role Playing" (TT No. 7)
Practice: Interview Project	20-25 minutes	
Follow On	5-10 minutes	
Evaluation of Session	10-15 minutes	
Total:	65-100 minutes	

ESTABLISHING GOOD RAPPORT (5-10 minutes). No matter how adroit the tutor nor how eager the learner, the tutoring experience may be unproductive unless the older and younger child feel at ease and comfortable with each other. Therefore, the first training sessions for tutors are designed to help them establish good rapport with the younger students.

Indicate to the teachers that two activities will be carried out to assist tutors and learners to develop comfortable relations: Socialization and Interviews. Though not oriented to tutoring techniques or subject matter, these activities produce the bond of mutual respect and comradeship on which a successful tutoring program is built. They are important activities and deserve serious attention from paired teachers.

SOCIALIZATION (5-10 minutes).* "Socialization" means getting the two paired classes acquainted with each other. It is a first step in developing a feeling of closeness between the two classes. The feeling should be fostered between all students in both classes and not limited to just a handful.

Before the next Workshop session, paired teachers will determine an activity in which students in the two classes can easily participate. The teachers will brief their respective classes ahead of time, conduct the activity with the two classes, and discuss the activity afterwards with their respective classes. Describe this process to the teachers in your group. Then pass out "Tutor/Learner Socialization" (TT No. 4). Run through that page and solict other ideas about possible two-class activities.

Also discuss with your group the tutor/teacher socialization mentioned at the bottom of the page. Indicate that teachers and tutors must establish a collaborative relationship and that it is important for teachers to take the lead toward this goal at the beginning of the tutor/teacher interactions.

INTERVIEW PROJECT (5-10 minutes). When the two whole classes get together for socialization activities, the students tend to interact as groups rather than as individuals. This helps to develop feelings of closeness between the two classes but needs to be augmented by individual contacts.

Once actual tutoring begins, tutors will work with learners on a one-to-one basis. The same tutor-learner pair stays together for a fairly long period. Therefore, tutors need to become acquainted with the younger students they will be working with regularly. This is the goal of the Interview project.

Describe this overall goal to your group. Then distribute "Interview Project" (TT No. 5). Go over the content of this page, encouraging members of your group to bring up questions. Next, pass out the sample "Interview Form" (TT No. 6). Tell your group that it contains questions tutors can ask learners and learners can ask tutors. Paired teachers should review these and see if there are other questions they would prefer using.

ROLE PLAYING AS A TECHNIQUE (15-20 minutes). Now ask members of your group to put aside the materials passed out earlier and consider with you a technique that is very effective in training situations: role playing. Indicate that role playing has three important benefits as part of training situations. *First*, role playing can show observers exactly what happens in a situation. Thus they can assess the effects of various interactions and can study the situation from different vantage points. *Second*, people can gain vicarious experience by playing a particular role ("Now I know how *he* must feel when that

---

*This activity does not apply to a peer-tutoring situation.

73

happens!"). This experience comes in handy when they meet the situation in the future. *Third*, role playing allows people to try out and practice new roles without risk of punishment for mistakes made while learning.

Pass out to the group "Steps in Role Playing" (TT No. 7). Read this over with them. Then tell them you are going to demonstrate role playing by having all of them participate.

PRACTICE: INTERVIEW PROJECT (20-25 minutes). Tell the group you are all going to role play the interview project. You act as "sending teacher," while they act as a "class." Go through the sequence a teacher should follow: remind class of earlier socialization; point out need to know more about the child they will work with; indicate that an interview is a good way to become better acquainted; tell them they will discuss the interview afterwards; go over interview form with them; have them practice asking questions of each other.

Discuss the role playing. Ask for comments on role playing, the particular roles played, and the interview questions.

FOLLOW ON (5-10 minutes). Tell your group that they will have two activities to arrange and conduct before the next Workshop session. The two paired teachers are to schedule and conduct at least one socialization activity, then they are to schedule and conduct the interview project. Remind the sending teacher that they should have their tutors role play the interview prior to doing it with the younger students. Remind the receiving teachers that they should brief their students on the purpose and nature of the two get-togethers.

EVALUATION OF THE SESSION (10-15 minutes). End the session with a short evaluation of it. This time, ask these questions of the group: How did this session improve over our last one? and What did each of you contribute to that improvement? Again, ask for specifics, and share your own evaluation with the group. Afterwards, write down the major points made during the evaluation.

Tutor/Learner Socialization

The two classes that are paired should have occasions in which the whole classes get together in order to become acquainted with one another. The classes can be combined with both teachers, or they can be split with each teacher having half of own and half of other class.

These get-togethers may be informal and social, or they may be a more structured activity. Some suggestions:

- Lunch in the park

- Field trip

- Art lesson

- Music lesson

- Simple writing lessons such as captions to drawings or photographs

- Special high-interest lesson using special interest or talent of one teacher

The goal of these socialization meetings is to increase the rapport between the two classes so that there is a feeling of "I know you" when they get together for tutoring.

Tutor/Teacher Socialization

During the socialization phase, it is advisable for the pair of teachers and tutors to meet in an informal setting once or twice. This may be for lunch or for refreshments after school.

The purpose is to develop a rapport upon which can be built the feeling of teamwork in their relationship.

Interview Project

This session has two objectives for the tutor: first, to develop a better understanding of younger children; second, to provide first-hand experience interacting with a younger child in school. The objectives basically are the same for the younger child: the understanding of and interacting with an older child. The younger and older children may interview each other during this session.

The younger and the older children will ask questions of each other to get better acquainted. They may draw pictures of each other as part of the session or as a follow-up.

Both classes should be carefully prepared for this session by role playing the interaction ahead of time. If this is done, take advantage of what is learned and discuss the process as it relates to going to another class.

The interviews will follow a sequence of questions, such as: "How old are you?" "How many brothers and sisters do you have?" "Do you have any pets?" "What are your hobbies?" The questions should help the tutor gain information that will be helping in tutoring.

For this session, the two classes could be split with each teacher having half of own class and half of other class.

Interview Form

Tutor ....

(Tutors should fill in answers to all questions.)

Tell your name. Tell why you are doing this. Make the child comfortable.

Ask for his help.

1. What is your name?

2. How old are you?

3. How do you look?

4. How many sisters do you have? How old are they?

5. How many brothers do you have? How old are they?

6. Do you have any pets? What kinds?

7. What is your favorite TV program?

8. What do you like to do in school?

9. What do you hate to do in school?

10. What kind of work do you do at home?

11. How do you feel about older kids?

12. How does your best friend feel about school?

13. How do you feel about school?

14. What is the most important thing you are going to do after school today?

Steps in Role Playing

1. Describe the situation in general.

2. Choose the actors.

3. Brief the actors as to their actions.

4. Assign tasks to the audience as observers.

5. Set up the scene, describing what each should do.

6. Start the action when all are ready.

7. Cut the interaction after the point has been illustrated.

8. Thank the actors, using their real names.

9. Discuss what was observed.

    a. Determine what happened.

    b. Ask the actors how they felt in the role.

    c. Explore what caused the situation to develop as it did.

    d. Focus on what could have been done differently.

Session III. More About Younger Students

Background: The last session dealt with the techniques of socialization, interviewing, and role playing. Teachers were to conduct at least one socialization activity and the interview project.

Purposes of Session: Enable teachers to help the tutors gain a better understanding, through observation, of the younger child with whom each is paired.

Familiarize tutors (through the teachers) with difficulties younger children have in learning.

Expose teachers to the brainstorming technique.

Agenda:

Topic	Approximate Time	Materials Required
Observation	5-10 minutes	"Observation" (TT No. 8) "Observing a Younger Student" (TT No. 9) (at least 2 for all teachers and tutors)
Difficulties of Learners	10-15 minutes	"Difficulties Children Have in Learning" (TT No. 10)
Brainstorming as a Technique	5-10 minutes	"Steps in Brainstorming (TT No. 11)
Practice: Brainstorming	25-30 minutes	Large sheets of paper, crayons, or marking pens
Follow On	5-10 minutes	
Evaluation of Session	10-15 minutes	Sheets of paper
Total:	60-90 minutes	

OBSERVATION (5-10 minutes).* Up to this point, the tutors-in-training have interacted with the entire receiving class and have begun to get acquainted with the younger student each will tutor. Now each tutor will get to know that student even better through an observation of him.

Introduce this idea to the teachers in your group. Distribute copies of "Observation" (TT No. 8). Go over that sheet with your group and elicit their reactions. Then pass out "Observing a Younger Student" and discuss the questions on it with your group. Note that the questions are intended to make it easy for the tutor to answer, requiring no writing if the tutor does not wish to write. Stress that tutors should *not* take the form with them when they observe, but rather should leave it in their own classroom and fill it out after they have come back from the observation. (It is distracting to younger students and their teachers to have a number of older students marking on their papers as they observe. Besides, the tutor should respond to the total situation and not just to transitory events.)

Receiving teachers must have their students engaged in an academic task when the tutors come to observe. If tutors observe during a free-time period, an art activity, or a discussion period, they will not learn much about their student. The most preferable situation is one in which the tutors observe their learners engaged in the academic area in which the tutoring will take place (i.e., math, spelling, etc.).

DIFFICULTIES OF LEARNERS (10-15 minutes). Now direct your teachers' attention to the next step in the training of tutors, a session in which the tutors examine reasons why young students have difficulty in school. Distribute copies of "Difficulties Children Have in Learning" (TT No. 10) and go over the contents with your group.

Point out that this is not an easy training session. Tutors are often reluctant to come up with reasons younger students have difficulty learning. Here the leader can assist tutors in two ways: ask them to refer to their observation forms for ideas about the difficulties their own learner seemed to be having; ask them to recall their own difficulties when they were younger.

Stress the importance of getting the tutors to develop potential solutions to the problems they identify. Tutors should not list a tedious catalog of difficulties younger children have in school unless they are given time to come up with ways these difficulties could be avoided, minimized, or overcome.

BRAINSTORMING AS A TECHNIQUE (5-10 minutes). Inform your group that one method of bringing out tutors' ideas is brainstorming. Remind them that they were using brainstorming during the first Workshop session when they came up with their hopes and concerns about intergrade tutoring.

Pass out copies of "Steps in Brainstorming" (TT No. 11). Go over the steps with the group. Tell them they will now try their hand at brainstorming.

PRACTICE: BRAINSTORMING (25-30 minutes). Divide the group into sub-groups, each of three or four members. Give each group some large sheets of paper and marking pens or crayons. Give each group a set of topics for them to brainstorm, such as:
- How to help a child feel important and successful
- Why children have problems learning in school
- Why teachers need tutors
- How to help a tutor feel successful

*"Observation" is not necessary when peer tutoring is being implemented.

86

In each group, have members take turns being the "leader" of a brainstorming session using one of the topics. For each topic, take three minutes to get out the ideas and two minutes to choose the best idea(s) for each topic.

Now bring the total group together. Have the persons responsible for each of the topics give only the best idea(s) for that topic. List them. It should be a powerful demonstration of the number of good ideas latent within people that can be unlocked in a short time.

FOLLOW ON (5-10 minutes). Tell your group they have two activities to complete between this session and the next one: conduct the observation, and conduct the session on difficulties of younger students. Remind them that the paired teachers will need to determine the time for the observation. They may want to set up multiple times so that not too many older students are observing at one time.

EVALUATION OF THE SESSION (10-15 minutes). To evaluate this session, pass out forms with two questions: "What can be done to improve these sessions?" and "How can I contribute to improving these sessions?" Have the members complete the forms immediately; collect them; ask someone to read the responses aloud while you write them on large sheets of paper. Ask the group to discuss the overall results. Keep track of comments that you can use in future sessions.

Observation

The tutors go to the younger students' classroom and observe the lower grade students while they are engaged in an instructional activity. The major purposes of this step are to give tutors first-hand exposure to: the kinds of problems younger students encounter in school, ways in which younger students behave in the classroom, and the teacher's need for help. It also allows the older students to become acquainted with the procedures and standards of the classroom in which they will be working.

This session should be purely observational. The older students should sit off to the side and just watch. Both the tutors and the learners must be prepared ahead of time. They should pay particular attention to getting data that will help them participate in these three training sessions: Difficulties Children Have in Learning, Ways to Help Younger Students Feel Important and Successful, and Understanding the Teacher's Role.

Observing a Younger Student

Tutor ....   Younger Child ....

1.   Was the child working well most of the time?

      YES   NO

2.   How did the child seem most of the time?

      HAPPY   UNHAPPY

3.   Did the teacher talk to or help the child very often?

      YES   NO

4.   How was the teacher most of the time?

      BUSY   NOT BUSY

5.   Write down anything special you observed:

Difficulties Children Have in Learning

This session has two objectives for the tutors: the first objective is to help the tutors diagnose learning difficulties of younger children; the second is to motivate tutors to learn techniques for helping younger students.

The tutors will use the information gained through observation as a basis for discussion. They may recall difficulties they had as a younger child. The teacher may have tutors act out situations as illustrations of difficulties. The teacher may have tutors draw their own pictures of a child they observed having difficulty. These pictures may also be used to stimulate discussion.

During the discussion the teacher should lead them to ask these kinds of questions:
- What is the nature of the problem?
- Why is he having this kind of problem?
- How can this problem be overcome?

The last question will set the stage for the next session. The teacher should end this session with the statement that next they won't be talking about the problems but ways in which the tutor can help a younger child to feel important and successful.

Steps in Brainstorming

1. Identify the topic for brainstorming. Write it at the top of a chalkboard or chart paper.

2. Ask for ideas.

3. Write the ideas on chalkboard or chart paper.

    • Take each contribution one at a time.

    • Repeat the essence using the contributor's words.

    • Check that you have understood what he meant.

    • Write using his words. Abbreviate, but check if meaning is conveyed.

4. List all ideas, *without discussion or evaluation*.

After brainstorming, the ideas may be organized, best ideas discussed, acted out, or permanently recorded, as appropriate to the purpose.

Session IV. About Tutoring and Teachers

Background: The last session focused on the techniques of observation and brainstorming. Teachers were to conduct the observation session. They were also to hold a session with tutors on difficulties younger children have in learning.

Purposes of Session: Review skill techniques of leading a discussion, role playing, and brainstorming, and identify successes and problems.

Familiarize tutors (through the teachers) with ways that younger children can feel important and successful.

Clarify the roles of the sending and receiving teachers in tutoring.

Agenda:

Topic	Approximate Time	Materials Required
The Skill Techniques	10-15 minutes	
Importance and Success	5-10 minutes	"Ways to Help Younger Students Feel Important and Successful" (TT No. 12)
Practice: Feeling Important and Successful	20-25 minutes	
Understanding the Teacher	10-15 minutes	"Understanding the Teacher's Role" (TT No. 13)
Follow On	5-10 minutes	
Evaluation of Session	10-15 minutes	
Total:	60-90 minutes	

THE SKILL TECHNIQUES (10-15 minutes). At the beginning of this Workshop session, review with the group the skill techniques they have dealt with so far: Leading a Discussion, Role Playing, and Brainstorming. Run through the three handouts for these skills with the group, but don't ask for comments. Ask these questions and discuss the answers:

1. Have you used the technique? If not, why not?
2. What successes can you identify?
3. What problems have you encountered?

IMPORTANCE AND SUCCESS (5-10 minutes). The next tutor training session to be conducted by the teachers is concerned with "Ways to Help Younger Students Feel Important and Successful." Pass out the sheet with that title (TT No. 12) and go over it with your group. Point out that this tutor training session will be in three parts: a review and discussion of ideas that came out of the previous session (on difficulties younger students have); brainstorming on ways to make younger students feel important and successful; and role playing the best ways identified from the brainstorming list.

PRACTICE: FEELING IMPORTANT AND SUCCESSFUL (20-25 minutes). Have the teachers in your group practice the session on helping younger students feel important and successful. Let them role-play tutors while you play the part of sending teacher. Go through all three stages of this session: discussion of ideas developed earlier; brainstorming to uncover ways of making the learners feel important and successful; and role playing some of the better ways.

UNDERSTANDING THE TEACHER (10-15 minutes). The final session in the general training of tutors will be devoted to their understanding of the teacher with whom they will be working. Pass out "Understanding the Teacher's Role" (TT No. 13) and discuss this with your group.

Allow for a good deal of discussion around this topic. Teachers tend to have problems seeing clearly their relationship with tutors. Sending teachers sometimes simply ignore the special role tutors play. This is inappropriate. Sending teachers must support the tutors and view them as colleagues going off to assist another colleague. Of even greater concern is the role of the receiving teacher. The receiving teacher is usually the closest to the tutors during the actual tutoring and must establish a good working relationship with them or little value will come from the tutoring. Your group will need to treat the tutor-teacher relationship at length to develop a good understanding of the interaction between tutor and teacher.

FOLLOW ON (5-10 minutes). Remind the teachers that they each will have a training session to complete before the next Workshop session: Ways to Help Youngsters Feel Important and Successful, and Understanding the Teacher.

EVALUATION OF THE SESSION (10-15 minutes). Conduct the evaluation of this session as you did the previous session. Have participants write answers to these questions: What did someone do today that facilitated our Workshop session? and What more could someone have done today to improve our Workshop session? Collect the papers, write out the answers for the entire group, and have the group discuss them.

Ways to Help Younger Students Feel
Important and Successful

This session has one primary objective for the tutors: to find as many ways as possible to give younger students a feeling of being appreciated, liked, useful, successful, important—to give the youngers a feeling that their wishes are being considered and that they are growing in skill.

The teacher should begin this session by reminding the tutors of some of their suggestions for reducing learning difficulties that came out of the previous session. The discussion should focus on whether the ways discussed would make a younger feel important and successful. They may relate their own experiences of what has made them feel that way as examples.

The teachers would then lead a brainstorming session to draw out from the tutors ways in which younger children can be made to feel important and successful.

The next step has the students choose the best ideas from the list and role play them. The emphasis should be on how the younger student would feel in the situation. The best ideas may be duplicated or put on a poster as reminders to the tutors when they begin to tutor.

Understanding the Teacher's Role

This tutor training session, normally conducted by the receiving teacher, has two objectives: to develop understanding of the teacher's role in the classroom and of the need for the tutors, and to promote cooperation between tutor and receiving teacher.

As discussion materials, the tutors will use the cases from the session on Difficulties Children Have in Learning and from their observation. The emphasis now is on the teacher's role in the situations. Questions:

- Did the teacher help or talk to the child having difficulty?
- Was the teacher busy most of the time?
- What might she feel about the child?
- What was the problem?
- How might the teacher feel about her ability to cope with the problem?

Discuss how the teacher is asking for help and how this is not a sign of inadequacy but a way of solving a problem. The teacher and the tutor working as a team, helping each other, can solve the problem of getting the child more attention and individual help.

Discuss the division of labor. The teacher's role is to diagnose needs and brief the tutor on what she would do if she had more time. She will help if things go wrong. She will be available to be asked for help. She will be interested in hearing the tutor's ideas about how to help the child.

The tutor's role is to be a friend and model as well as to provide specific help. This has responsibilities. The teacher and especially the younger student are depending on the tutor. The tutor has the advantages of time and the nearness of age to be a special kind of help. The challenge is there of finding new ways to help.

Tutors may role-play some situations, with the receiving teacher playing herself. For example:

- Ways to make teachers feel important, successful, useful, etc.
- How to ask for help.
- How to give information about your child.
- How to offer ideas you would like to try.
- What to do if your child will not behave.

Session V. Specific Tutoring Procedures

Background: The last session dealt with making younger children feel important and successful, and the role of the teacher during tutoring. Teachers were to hold one session on each topic with their tutors. Teachers should also be familiar with the school's Tutoring Procedures, which form the basis for this Workshop.

Purposes of Session: Review, demonstration, and practice of specific tutoring procedures.

Agenda:

Topic	Approximate Time	Materials Required
Requirements for a Well-Trained Tutor	5-10 minutes	
Review of Tutoring Procedures	10-15 minutes	School's Tutoring Procedures (set for each pair of teachers)
Demonstration of Tutoring	15-20 minutes	
Practice: Tutoring Procedures	15-20 minutes	
Follow On	5-10 minutes	"Training Students for Specific Procedures" (TT No. 14), "Reinforcement Procedures" (TT No. 15)
Evaluation of Session	10-15 minutes	Sheets of paper
Total:	60-90 minutes	

REQUIREMENTS FOR A WELL-TRAINED TUTOR (5-10 minutes). At the start of this Workshop session, go over with your group the requirements for a well-trained tutor:

1. The tutor knows exactly with which learner he will work.
2. The tutor knows the objectives his learner is to achieve.
3. The tutor knows something about the kinds of problems his learner has had.
4. The tutor knows some techniques for overcoming those problems.
5. The tutor knows how to help the learner feel important and successful.
6. The tutor understands his relationship with the receiving teacher.
7. The tutor knows the procedures he is to use as he works with his learner.

Most of these requirements have been met already as a result of the previous training session with the tutors. The critical requirements that remains is number 7: exactly what a tutor is to do when he sits down to work with his younger student.

REVIEW OF THE TUTORING PROCEDURES (10-15 minutes). This session assumes that you and your teachers have mastered the material on your school's tutoring procedures.

Have the members of your group review the tutoring procedures that you have chosen to use. Take them through all the steps, including examination of materials. Answer any questions that are asked for clarification ("Should that book be open at all times?") but turn aside questions that require speculative answers ("Why would a tutor have difficulty with step 9?"). Also, avoid any discussion at this point. Tell your group that they will be dealing with the tutoring procedures later on in the session. Now you simply want to re-acquaint them with the procedures.

DEMONSTRATION OF TUTORING (15-20 minutes). Pick two members of your group to work with you in a demonstration of tutoring. (Choose people who have shown a facility for role playing.) Ask one of them to play the role of younger learner and one to play the role of receiving teacher. Indicate that you will be playing the role of tutor.

Demonstrate the tutoring procedures. Include everything: walk through the door and greet the "teacher," greet your "learner," go through a few warmup comments and questions, then begin the actual tutoring. Play it straight: don't be silly and don't interrupt the tutoring for asides to your audience. Be sure to commit a few errors, so your "teacher" can observe them, correct them on the spot, or note them down for later discussion.

After the demonstration, discuss it briefly with the total group. Again, attempt to respond only to questions calling for clarification ("Why did you do *that*?") and avoid speculative questions or ones that challenge the tutoring procedures ("I really don't think we should do that with our children."). This is not the time to revise the tutoring procedures. That will be done after you have had enough experience with the procedures to see where revisions are needed and what form they should take.

PRACTICE: TUTORING PROCEDURES (15-20 minutes). Have your teacher pairs role play the tutoring process. Emphasize that this will help familiarize them with the procedures and aid them in demonstrating to tutors. The first time through, have the sending teachers play tutor and the receiving teachers play learner. You play receiving teacher. Send the "tutors" out of the room through the entire tutoring procedures, touching every step although shortening the time for the lengthier ones.

After enough time, have them change roles and begin again. This is valuable because it allows the sending teacher to see the tutoring process through the eyes of a younger student, and allows the receiving teacher to realize the demands the tutoring procedures place on the tutors.

Following this second practice session, ask the group if there are any other questions. By this time the questions should have dwindled to minor ones, and it is likely that the discussion of tutoring procedures will be short. Ask the teachers to report how they felt as tutor and as learner.

FOLLOW ON (5-10 minutes). During the time between this session and the next one, the *receiving* teachers are to conduct training with the tutors on the specific tutoring procedures. Largely the training will be accomplished as was demonstrated in the present Workshop session: a role playing demonstration for the tutors, then their role playing of the procedures between themselves. Pass out "Training Tutors for Specific Procedures" (TT No. 14) and "Reinforcement Procedures" (TT No. 15). Indicate to your teachers that they should plan on a number of sessions, since tutors will need a fair amount of practice before they can be called fully trained.

EVALUATION OF THE SESSION (10-15 minutes). Have the members of your group evaluate the session by answering these two open-ended questions: Today's Workshop was valuable to me because _____; and Today's Workshop was a disappointment to me because _____. Collect the papers (which should be submitted anonymously), summarize the results, and discuss them.

Training Tutors for Specific Procedures

This step in the tutor training involves more than one session, and has three objectives: to give tutors an overview of the learners' objectives, the materials to be used, and the procedures in tutoring; to give tutors practice in the tutoring procedures; to introduce and give practice in effective reinforcement procedures to use with learners. These sessions are the responsibility of the receiving teacher.

At the first session the teacher will discuss the classroom program in the subject that tutoring will take place, the overall objectives, and those particular objectives with which the tutors will be working. She will show them the materials the learners will be using and provide an opportunity for the tutors to become familiar with how the learner uses them. The tutors will learn what correct responses to expect from the learners.

At the end of this session the teacher will introduce the tutors to the type of reinforcement she will expect from them as they work with the learners (see "Reinforcement Procedures"). She will draw upon their previous experiences in Socialization and Interviewing to remind them how to establish a friendly atmosphere. At this time the focus will be on how to handle correct and incorrect responses, and how to encourage independence in the learner. The teacher will demonstrate the procedures with herself as tutor and one tutor as learner. The tutors can then pair up, read to each other, and practice making correct responses as a tutor. The teacher will observe, give support, and offer suggestions. This session should end with the anticipation that at their next meeting they will learn more procedures to help their learner master the objectives.

The second session begins with a review of the reinforcement procedures. The teacher then demonstrates the total daily tutoring sequence, again acting out the role of tutor. The tutors will pair up and role play the procedures, acting in turn as both tutor and learner. The teacher may want the tutors to practice only parts of the total sequence at first, and then practice all the parts together.

This role playing practice may continue for several sessions until the tutors become familiar with the procedures and the use of the materials. The teacher needs to observe closely, and give feedback and support frequently to the tutors. Reinforcement procedures should be continually stressed. (Do not continue this practice too long because the tutors will be anxious to get started.)

When the receiving teacher feels comfortable, she should set a date to begin and establish a time before that date for one session on Clinicing. The tutors should know that at the next session they will discuss how she will continue to help them be successful tutors.

Reinforcement Procedures

A.   Establishing a Friendly Atmosphere.

The tutor will first need to establish a friendly relationship with the learner.

This will be stressed in all socialization activities as well as in tutoring. The tutor should be reminded to:
1.   Call the learner by name.
2.   Smile.
3.   Act friendly.
4.   Sit next to learner.

B.   Supporting the Learner During Tutoring.

At every step of the tutoring procedures the key to success lies in the kind of reinforcement the tutor gives the learner. Continuous attention by the tutor while he is with the learner is vital. These procedures should be stressed:
1.   Praise correct responses regularly.
2.   Mark correct responses, if appropriate.
3.   Help with errors in a positive manner.
   a.   Emphasize the question, not the wrong answer.
   b.   Ask the question again.
   c.   Help find the answer.

C.   Encouraging Independence in the Learner.

As a successful working relationship is established the tutor should become aware of ways to encourage independence in the learner. These procedures should be introduced at the beginning of tutoring and stressed increasingly as tutoring goes on:
1.   Help the learner find the answers instead of giving them to him.
2.   Praise the learner for following steps without being told, such as:
   a.   Asking questions.
   b.   Turning pages, marking answers, etc.
   c.   Locating information.
   d.   Studying independently in an area of need.

Session VI. Ongoing Support for Tutors

Background: Teachers and tutors have now been trained in all fundamentals of tutoring. Since the last Workshop session, receiving teachers were to practice tutoring techniques with their tutors.

Purposes of Session: Lay the groundwork for weekly meetings (clinics) between teachers and tutors.

Familiarize teachers with tutor observation and feedback.

Agenda:

Topic	Approximate Time	Materials Required
The Clinic	10-15 minutes	"Clinicing" (TT No. 16)
Observing Tutoring	10-15 minutes	"Tutor Observation Form" (TT No. 17) (enough for weekly evaluation of all tutors)
Practice: Observing and Clinicing	25-30 minutes	"Teacher-Tutor Meeting (Clinicing)" (TT No. 18)
Evaluation of Workshop	15-20 minutes	"Workshop Evaluation Form" (TT No. 19)
Total:	60-80 minutes	

THE CLINIC (10-15 minutes). Once tutors have completed their training in the specific tutoring procedures they are to use, it is easy to assume that their training is completed. That is not so, a point you will have to make forcefully to the teachers in your group. Training and support of tutors must be an ongoing process for two important reasons. First, tutors need to review the tutoring procedures because they will forget some or become slipshod in their application. Second, as modifications to the tutoring procedures are worked out, tutors will need additional training in them. The clinic is the vehicle for conducting the ongoing training and support of tutors.

Remind your teachers of the provision for regular teacher-tutor meetings. These regular meetings are called clinics, and the process of the meetings is called "clinicing." Pass out copies of "Clinicing" (TT No. 16) and go over it with your group. Call their attention to one important point: before tutoring begins, teachers will hold a training session with tutors to discuss the concept and purpose of the weekly clinic.

OBSERVING TUTORING (10-15 minutes). Now go over with your group the role of the receiving teacher during tutoring. Classroom teachers are integral to effective intergrade tutoring. They must follow through on their unique assignments if tutoring is to go well. As shown in the Sample Tutoring Procedures (page 130), classroom teachers work along with the tutors when tutoring is in process, providing immediate assistance to tutors and learners when needed. Another important role the teacher fills is that of monitor, who carefully observes the tutoring and records unusual occurrences. One part of this monitoring is carried out by completing a Tutor Observation Form for each tutor regularly.

Pass out copies of the "Tutor Observation Form" (TT No. 17) and go over it. The questions are easy for the teacher to answer, calling for yes-no responses. Note that teachers observe both the tutors' general skills and their specific tutoring procedures. Indicate that the form provides space for general observations.

Classroom teachers are to observe each tutor frequently—once a week if possible—and to complete a form for each tutor. The teacher brings these forms to the weekly tutor-teacher clinic and uses them to give tutors accurate feedback on their behavior.

PRACTICE: OBSERVING AND CLINICING (25-30 minutes). Divide the group into sub-groups with four members. In each sub-group, have two teachers role-play tutoring while the other two observe and complete a Tutor Observation Form. Then have the teachers reverse roles so that all four can observe and record observations.

Next, pass out copies of "Teacher-Tutor Meeting (Clinicing)" (TT No. 18) and go over it. Then have the members of each sub-group hold a clinic, with teachers taking turns acting as the leader of the meeting, while the other role play tutors.

EVALUATION OF THE WORKSHOP (15-20 minutes). Ask the teachers in your group to evaluate the Workshop as a whole. Pass out the "Workshop Evaluation Form" (TT No. 19) and have them complete it immediately. Collect the papers and tally the responses. Then hold a discussion on the results of the evaluation. Be sure that you share with the group your own reactions and evaluations.

FOLLOW ON. The Workshop is now completed. Although the rest of the program—the tutoring itself—has yet to begin, congratulate the teachers on reaching this important threshold. Tell the teachers in your group that they now have three assignments: conduct the training session for tutors on the clinic; begin tutoring; and observe tutors in action. Also they will be following the regular sequence of meeting regularly with their paired teacher, meeting regularly as a group, and meeting regularly with their tutors.

A successful tutoring program is about to get under way in your school.

Clinicing (First Session)

This session has five objectives for the tutor:

1. To give tutors techniques for helping each other in teacher-tutor meetings.
2. Legitimize using each other as resources in solving problems.
3. Provide opportunity for skills practice.
4. Give tutors some diagnostic skills.
5. Give the teacher the opportunity to function as a resource person.

The receiving teacher will work with the tutors on problems they may have. The tutors offer suggested solutions and discuss the merits in terms of helping the child. The tutors may act out problems and solutions and get other suggestions for doing it better.

The tutors should learn to ask these questions in diagnosing and solving problems:

1. What difficulty is the learner having? Why?
2. What needs to happen for him to succeed?
3. What does he need to learn to do a better job?
4. How can I help him feel good about where he is now and at the same time encourage him to learn to do better?

At this time the teacher can have the tutors go through a final practice of tutoring before they begin. She can use this opportunity to give feedback that will help and support regarding the practice session.

The receiving teacher should tell the tutors that the present session is a practice for weekly teacher-tutor clinics.

The teacher should also indicate that when the two teachers are observing, they are there as friends to help tutors be successful. Assure the tutors that all problems will be discussed with the tutors afterwards. Show the tutors a copy of the Tutor Observation Form.

This session should be held just before tutoring begins. Not more than a week of tutoring should take place before the regular teacher-tutor clinics begin.

Tutor Observation Form

Yes ..... No ..... A. Does tutor ESTABLISH A FRIENDLY ATMOSPHERE? (Call learner by name, smile, act friendly.)

Yes ..... No ..... B. Does tutor SUPPORT LEARNER? (Praise for correct answers, handle errors positively.)

Yes ..... No ..... C. Does tutor ENCOURAGE INDEPENDENCE in learner? (Help find answer instead of giving it, praise the learner for following steps without being told.)

Yes ..... No ..... D. Does tutor TAKE RESPONSIBILITY? (Deal with problems, come on time, aware of his own strengths and weaknesses, ask for help when necessary.)

Yes ..... No ..... E. Does tutor FOLLOW TUTORING STEPS?

Tutor strengths: ....
....
....

Training/Improvement Needed: ....
....
....
....

Comments: ....
....
....
....

Teacher-Tutor Meeting (Clinicing)

This session is to be held on a weekly basis and is the essential ingredient in a successful long-term teacher-tutor relationship.

The paired teachers meet with tutors to:

1.   Discuss the purpose of the session.

2.   Air the tutors' concerns and problems.

3.   Air the teachers' concerns and problems.

4.   Discuss/brainstorm/role play solutions to the problems.

5.   Give positive feedback, support, and encouragement to the tutors.

6.   Give additional training.

The teachers should apply the "Steps in Leading a Discussion," page 65, keeping the focus on mutual problem-solving instead of finding blame or reasons why improvement cannot be made.

Workshop Evaluation Form

Directions: For items 1-6 please give candid answers to the statements.

Do *not* sign your name. Mark each item by circling one of the choices:

SA = Strongly Agree with the statement

A = Agree

N = Neither agree nor disagree

D = Disagree

SD = Strongly Disagree with the statement

1.	The Workshop was well organized.	SA	A	N	D	SD
2.	The Workshop presentations were interesting.	SA	A	N	D	SD
3.	The content of the Workshop was valuable to me.	SA	A	N	D	SD
4.	The Workshop was a good use of my time.	SA	A	N	D	SD
5.	I learned a lot from the Workshop.	SA	A	N	D	SD
6.	I am now ready to begin tutoring.	SA	A	N	D	SD

The most outstanding feature of the Workshop was ....
....
....

The weakest feature of the Workshop was ....
....
....

I could use more guidance in ....
....
....

The following is an exemplary tutoring procedure for decoding skills in reading. It has proved particularly successful when used as the basic tutoring procedure with teachers and tutors new to tutoring. Once teachers and tutors have become familiar and facile with this basic procedure, schools have been able to build upon it to expand their program to meet the needs of their students more completely. Some expansions are the product of systematic efforts by teachers; others result from the ingenuity and creativity of individual tutors.

This basic procedure forms a sequence in which tutors can be trained readily and will experience progress with younger learners. If later expansions meet with limited success, tutors and teachers can always return to the basics while reworking the expansions. School personnel have discovered that inaugurating tutoring with this basic procedure is rewarding to all involved and gets tutoring off to a healthy beginning.

These sample procedures are only one way to conduct tutoring. While the procedures are for decoding skills in reading, the scheme employed can be used as a model for many other content areas.

COGNITIVE OBJECTIVES

The following objectives are established:

Sight Vocabulary Development. The student will be able to read correctly the words contained in the assigned reading text.

Word Attack Skills. When a student encounters a word that is not a part of his sight vocabulary repertoire, he will be able to attack the word and correctly read it.

Simple Comprehension Skills. The student will be able to answer correctly literal questions concerning the content of passages in his reading text.

EVALUATION PROCEDURES

To measure *sight vocabulary development*, the student is asked to read a list of words that are used in his reading text, such as the words listed in the back of basal reading texts. The number of words missed is scored.

For *word attack skills*, the student is asked to read a passage in his reading text that he has not previously read. The teacher rates the effectiveness of the student in attacking words not a part of the student's sight vocabulary repertoire.

To assess *simple comprehension skills*, the teacher has the student read a passage in his reading text, then asks questions about the content of the passage (e.g., "Who is talking?" "Where did the action take place?" "What happened at the end?"). The teacher judges the adequacy of answers.

TUTORING MATERIALS

Materials required for tutoring include standard school supplies (reading texts, blank flashcards, pencils, and paper), items to be included in a Tutor Kit, and certain support materials. Tutor Kit and support materials need to be prepared by the school. These latter items are marked with an asterisk and samples are found on pages 131-139.

The Tutor Kit. Each tutor is provided a folder to hold tutoring materials. This can be made locally with a manila folder fastened inside a larger construction paper cover or can be a commercial version available at stationers. The following items are placed in the folder:

*Tutoring Steps	A simplified list of steps in the daily sequence as a reminder to tutors.
*Word List	A form for the tutor to record words missed by the learner during reading.
*Daily Log	Used by tutors for recording activities, evaluations of tutoring sessions, and items to be discussed with the teacher.
Flashcards	Tutors make flashcards for words missed and recorded on the Word List. These are kept in pockets or envelopes fastened to a page in the folder.
Blank paper	For tutors to use when the need arises during a tutoring session.

Support Materials. Two forms are used by teachers:

*Tutor Skills Checklist	For the sending teacher's use to record mastery of prerequisite skills by tutors.
*Tutor Observation Form	To guide the teacher's observation of tutors while they are tutoring.

TUTORING PROCEDURES

The tutor works with his learner by listening to him read, helping him attack new words, helping him study sight vocabulary words, and asking him questions about what has been read.

The learner receives *appropriate practice* when he sight-reads words in the text and on flashcards, when he attacks unknown words encountered in the text, and when he answers questions about material he has read.

The learner receives *sufficient practice* when the tutor gives him enough trials, using a variety of materials and procedures, for him to master objectives.

The learner receives *knowledge of results* from the tutor's regular reinforcement of correct responses and from the teacher's feedback on his evaluations.

*Samples are on pages 131-139.

The tutor follows this sequence on a daily basis:

Word Study
↓
Reading
↓
Questioning-Discussing
↓
Record-keeping

Word Study. Before reading, the tutor and learner study the flashcards made out during previous sessions. The tutor shows the flashcards to the learner, one at a time, and asks him to read each one. After questioning-discussing, the tutor and learner make out flashcards for words missed during reading that day. The learner reads the words missed that day from the Word List and spells them to the tutor who makes out the flashcards. Then the two students review the flashcards following the same procedures described above.

Reading. Before the learner begins reading from the text, he turns to the appropriate page and reviews what was read previously. He and the tutor discuss the content of pages read (who are the characters, what has happened, etc.) and anticipate the coming pages (Tutor: "What do you think will happen next?"). Then the learner reads while the tutor listens carefully.

1. The learner holds the book and turns pages himself.

2. The tutor helps with any words that give the learner difficulty. He has the learner sound out the words, following a word attack procedure preferred by the teacher. Then the tutor has the learner spell the word while the tutor writes it on the Word List. Finally, the tutor has the learner re-read the sentence in which the missed word occurred.

3. When five new words have been added to the Word List (or when about 10 minutes remain in the tutoring period) the tutor and learner stop reading for the day.

Questioning-Discussing. When the actual reading period has ended, the tutor asks the learner questions about the content of the material read that day. The two students discuss the content, relating it to other material read and to events in their own lives.

Record-keeping. In the final minutes of the session the tutor fills out the Daily Log. He records pages read that day, evaluates the session, and comments on the learner's progress and needs.

PREREQUISITE TUTOR SKILLS

The sending teacher diagnoses the tutors' mastery of skills needed in tutoring, using observation or a simple teacher-made test. Results are recorded on the Tutor Skills Checklist. If required, the sending teacher trains individual tutors on:

1. Correct pronunciation of letter sounds, particularly long and short vowel sounds.

2. Recognition of letter names.

3. Manuscript writing (printing).

THE TEACHERS' ROLE

In this approach to intergrade tutoring two teachers are paired and work closely together. One is an upper-grade teacher who sends tutors, and the other is a primary-grade teacher who receives tutors.

A six-session Workshop on tutoring is presented for teachers who will be participating in the program. The Workshop prepares teachers to successfully conduct tutoring. During the Workshop the paired teachers plan the details of their own tutoring. Then they train older students in tutoring procedures.

During actual tutoring sessions the teachers play an active part. They circulate throughout the room observing tutoring in action, helping students with difficulties, and praising students for work done well.

Regularly the paired teachers get together to review their tutoring program and make needed modifications. Each week the teachers meet with their tutors to solve problems and provide retraining. Once in a while all participating teachers meet to share ideas and decide on future actions.

Tutoring Steps

SMILE!   BE FRIENDLY!   USE FIRST NAMES!

PRAISE!!   HELP!!

1. REVIEW word cards.

    STUDY missed words.

2. DISCUSS story.

3. LISTEN to child read.

4. HELP with missed words.

    SOUND OUT word.

    WRITE word on Word List.

    Child READS word again in sentence.

After 5 new words on Word List . . .

5. ASK questions about story.

    "What happened?"

    "Who was in the story?"

    "What sentence goes with this picture?"

6. MAKE flashcards for new words.

    STUDY new words.

7. FILL OUT Daily Log.

Word List

WORD	PAGE	WORD	PAGE

Tutor's Daily Log

_____   _____
Learner   Tutor

MONDAY	TUESDAY	WEDNESDAY	THURSDAY	FRIDAY

Things to talk about with teacher ....
....
....
....

Directions for use of DAILY LOG.

Date		◄——— EVALUATION OF SESSION

+ Very Good

= OK

- Not Good, Discuss problem
  with child and teacher.

135

Tutor Skills Checklist

<table>
<tr><td rowspan="3">Tutor's Name</td><td colspan="3">Correct Pronunciation</td><td rowspan="3">Knows Letter Names</td><td rowspan="3">Clear Manuscript Printing</td></tr>
<tr><td>long vowels</td><td>short vowels</td><td>consonants</td></tr>
<tr><td></td><td></td><td></td></tr>
<tr><td></td><td></td><td></td><td></td><td></td><td></td></tr>
<tr><td></td><td></td><td></td><td></td><td></td><td></td></tr>
<tr><td></td><td></td><td></td><td></td><td></td><td></td></tr>
<tr><td></td><td></td><td></td><td></td><td></td><td></td></tr>
<tr><td></td><td></td><td></td><td></td><td></td><td></td></tr>
<tr><td></td><td></td><td></td><td></td><td></td><td></td></tr>
<tr><td></td><td></td><td></td><td></td><td></td><td></td></tr>
<tr><td></td><td></td><td></td><td></td><td></td><td></td></tr>
<tr><td></td><td></td><td></td><td></td><td></td><td></td></tr>
<tr><td></td><td></td><td></td><td></td><td></td><td></td></tr>
<tr><td></td><td></td><td></td><td></td><td></td><td></td></tr>
<tr><td></td><td></td><td></td><td></td><td></td><td></td></tr>
<tr><td></td><td></td><td></td><td></td><td></td><td></td></tr>
<tr><td></td><td></td><td></td><td></td><td></td><td></td></tr>
<tr><td></td><td></td><td></td><td></td><td></td><td></td></tr>
<tr><td></td><td></td><td></td><td></td><td></td><td></td></tr>
<tr><td></td><td></td><td></td><td></td><td></td><td></td></tr>
<tr><td></td><td></td><td></td><td></td><td></td><td></td></tr>
</table>

Recording: +   mastery

              -     needs to study (change to + when achieves mastery)

Tutor Observation Form

Sending Teacher ....

Receiving Teacher ....

Tutor ....   Date ....

A. Does tutor ESTABLISH A FRIENDLY ATMOSPHERE?   Yes   No
    (Call learner by name, smile, act friendly)

B. Does tutor SUPPORT LEARNER? (Praise, correct answers,   Yes   No
    handle errors positively)

C. Does tutor ENCOURAGE INDEPENDENCE in learner?   Yes   No
    (Help find answer instead of giving it, praise the learner for
    following the steps without being told)

D. Does tutor TAKE RESPONSIBILITY? (Deal with problems,   Yes   No
    come on time, aware of his own strengths and weaknesses,
    ask for help when necessary)

E. Does tutor FOLLOW TUTORING STEPS? (Word study,   Yes   No
    reading, questioning, record-keeping)

Tutor Strengths: ....
....
....
. ...

Training/Improvement Needed: . ...
....
....
....

Comments: ....
....
....

To grow in effectiveness, tutoring should be evaluated at the end of each cycle and the results used to make decisions about the program. The basic rationale for the evaluation is to provide feedback for program improvement.

A simple five-step model for program evaluation has been used by schools. The model has proven useful in developing effective tutoring programs in those schools.

1. *Establish Objectives and Procedures.* The school determines the objectives for tutoring and the procedures to be used to reach those objectives.

2. *Prepare Evaluation Instruments.* Two kinds of instruments are prepared that address achievement of objectives: those that measure the achievement of cognitive objectives, and those that assess participants' reactions to the program.

Sample instruments are on pages 143-149. They include a Learner Evaluation Form (in the area of decoding skills in reading), a Learner Questionnaire, a Tutor Questionnaire, and a Teacher Questionnaire. A description of their use and scoring is also provided. Some instruments may be used in the same form for end-of-cycle evaluations; others may be changed to measure particular program features at different times of the year.

3. *Collect and Summarize Data.* The various evaluation instruments are administered to appropriate people and collected. The Tutoring Coordinator scores them and prepares a summary of the data, pointing out strengths and deficiencies.

4. *Discuss Results and Make Decisions.* The Tutoring Coordinator and participating teachers review the summarized data. They discuss ways of building on strengths and overcoming deficiencies. Finally, decisions are made concerning modifications in the next tutoring cycle. This includes preparing new instruments to evaluate the modifications.

5. *Report Results and Decisions.* The Tutoring Coordinator reports the results of the evaluation and the decisions made concerning tutoring to the entire staff and to parents.

The time span for an end-of-cycle evaluation is two weeks, assuming steps 1 and 2 are completed prior to the two-week period. During the first week steps 3 and 4 are carried out: data are collected, summarized, discussed, and decisions are made. Actions required by the decisions are conducted the second week, such as preparing new materials and retraining tutors. Step 5, reporting results and decisions, can be accomplished any time shortly after the two-week evaluation period. Tutoring does not go on during the two-week period to provide time for staff members to successfully conduct the evaluation.

Learner Evaluation Form

yes ✓

Teacher ....

Grade ....

Student Names	Book	Page	Vocabulary	Word Attack	Comprehension (3 questions)
......					
......					
......					
......					
......					
......					
......					
......					
......					
......					
......					
......					
......					
......					
......					
......					
......					
......					
......					

Key for Recording Results

Vocabulary	*Word Attack*	*Comprehension*
E: (excellent) 0 words missed	E: attacks words successfully	E: 0 errors
G: (good) 1 or 2 words missed	G: attacks words unsuccessfully	G: 1 error
P: (poor) 3 or more words missed	P: no word attack	P: 2 or 3 errors

Learner Questionnaire

1. Do you like to read with a tutor?

    YES   NO

2. Is your tutor friendly?

    YES   NO

3. Do you want our class to continue with the tutoring program?

    YES   NO

4. Do you want to change and have a different tutor?

    YES   NO

5. Do you think tutoring has helped you to be a better reader?

    YES   NO

6. Do you like to read?

    YES   NO

Tutor Questionnaire

1.   Were you given enough training to be a good tutor?

      Yes   Not Sure   No

2.   How do you get along with the student you tutor?

      Good   Fair   Poor

3.   How do you get along with the teachers in the tutoring?

      Good   Fair   Poor

4.   Has tutoring helped *you* in school?

      Yes   Not Sure   No

5.   Have you helped the student you tutor in *his* school work?

      Yes   Not Sure   No

6.   How do your parents feel about you being a tutor?

      They Like It   Not Sure   They Don't Like It

7.   Overall, how do you feel about tutoring?

      It's Good   It's OK   It's Bad

8.   What's the thing you like *best* about tutoring?

9.   What's the thing you like *least* about tutoring?

Teacher Questionnaire

1. How effective was the workshop in preparing you for tutoring?

    Effective   Ineffective
        A   B   C   D

2. How effective were the training procedures for preparing tutors?

    Effective   Ineffective
        A   B   C   D

3. How useful are your clinics with tutors for solving problems and giving tutors additional training?

    Useful   Useless
        A   B   C   D

4. How useful are your meetings with your paired teacher for examining and developing your program?

    Useful   Useless
        A   B   C   D

5. How useful are periodic sharing meetings involving all teachers implementing tutoring?

    Useful   Useless
        A   B   C   D

6. How much academic growth have you seen in students in *your* class?

    Much   None
        A   B   C   D

7. How much social/affective growth have you seen in students in *your* class?

    Much   None
        A   B   C   D

8. How much academic growth have you seen in students in your *paired* class?

    Much   None
        A   B   C   D

9. How much social/affective growth have you seen in students in your *paired* class?

    Much   None
        A   B   C   D

10. How much support and help in solving problems have you received from the Tutoring Coordinator?

    Much   None
        A   B   C   D

11. How much support and help in solving problems have you received from the principal?

    Much   None
        A   B   C   D

12. Overall, how do you rate the tutoring program?

    Excellent   Poor
        A   B   C   D

13. Describe the one major benefit you have seen from the tutoring program.

14. Describe the one most serious concern you feel should be overcome regarding the tutoring program.

USING THE EVALUATION FORMS

Learner Evaluation Form. On this form the classroom teacher records the results of individual assessment of students. First the teacher records the student's name, the book he is currently reading, and the page on which he is then reading. Next the teacher has the child go back two pages and read aloud to her; in the column headed "Vocabulary" the teacher indicates how many words the child misreads. Then the teacher has the child turn ahead two pages beyond where he is reading; under the column headed "Word Attack" she indicates how well the student attacks unknown words. Finally, the teacher asks the child three questions concerning the material just read; under the column "Comprehension" she indicates how well he answered the three questions.

By assigning numerical weights of 3 for excellent, 2 for good, and 1 for poor, averages can be computed for each skill area, for total reading skills, and for individual students.

Learner Questionnaire. Teachers whose students receive tutoring have their students complete this form by circling Yes or No for each question. The teacher reads the questions aloud for the children, and verifies that they are answering the appropriate items.

Scoring is the tally of the number of students choosing each answer for each question.

Tutor Questionnaire. Teachers have their students who are tutors complete this form by circling an answer for each item.

Scoring is the tally of the number of students choosing each answer for each question. For items 8 and 9, all comments are recorded on a master tally sheet.

Teacher Questionnaire. All participating teachers complete this form by circling the answer of their choice for each item.

Scoring is accomplished by assigning numerical weights of 4 for A, 3 for B, 2 for C, and 1 for D, and calculating averages for each item. Any average below 2.5 is considered negative; one at 2.5 or larger is considered positive. All comments for items 13 and 14 are recorded on a master list.

OVERVIEW

Interschool tutoring is the process by which secondary school students (from junior and senior high schools) tutor elementary school students. While interschool tutoring follows the general pattern of tutoring described earlier, there are enough unique features to warrant a separate treatment.

An interschool tutoring program provides tutorial assistance to older elementary school students who would not be able to receive it if tutoring were limited to students within an elementary school. In most elementary schools there are students in upper grades who could benefit from the help of an older tutor, and secondary schools are the logical places to locate such tutors.

Evaluations of interschool tutoring have shown pronounced growth for both tutors and learners. Frequently the gains made by older tutors in academic skills have exceeded those of the students receiving tutoring. Tutoring has had two additional benefits for the older students: it provides an outlet for the social service interests that develop in teenagers, and it serves as a motivating force for some students who have begun to lose interest in schooling.

MODELS FOR INTERSCHOOL TUTORING

Two basic approaches to interschool tutoring have been used. In one the secondary students choose tutoring as an elective class for which they receive credit. In the second, tutoring is integrated into a "regular" class, typically English. In both cases a secondary school teacher is assigned to work with the students, including accompanying them when they go to the elementary school for tutoring.

In the elective-class approach, students tutor four days a week and on the fifth day they share experiences and prepare materials. Grades are given strictly on the basis of the students' adherence to the requirements and responsibilities of the tutoring program.

In the "regular" class approach, tutoring is conducted three days a week, with the other two days devoted to work in the academic subject area of the class. Tutors are expected to complete the same amount of work ordinarily required for the class, and grades are given on the basis of both tutoring and academic work. The tutoring experience is integrated with the coursework, for example having tutors maintain diaries and write reports of their experiences.

STEPS IN IMPLEMENTATION

1. *Establish Contact.* Usually, teachers at the elementary school have defined a need for secondary school tutors. The elementary school then contacts a nearby junior or senior high school and describes its need for older tutors. Administrators of the two schools meet to decide if an interschool tutoring program would benefit their students.

2. *Recruit the Secondary School Teacher.* If the two schools agree on the value of interschool tutoring, the secondary school administrator recruits a teacher to lead the class by finding a volunteer who is enthusiastic about tutoring.

3. *Recruit Elementary Teachers.* The elementary school now decides which particular classes will receive the tutors and which students are to be tutored. Some considerations are whether to tutor an entire class vs. the most needy students in a number of classes, what grade levels to select, etc. After making the decisions, appropriate teachers are recruited.

4. *Develop a Plan*. Once all participating teachers have been recruited, the secondary school teacher and the elementary school's Tutoring Coordinator plan the program. The plan includes the days of the week and the time of tutoring, tutors' transportation (if necessary), academic area for tutoring, methods for evaluating program effectiveness, when and where tutor training will be done, and schedule of tutoring cycles.

5. *Recruit Tutors*. Next, the secondary school recruits students to be tutors. This can be done by "advertising" the program on bulletin boards and through presentations to eligible students. Since participation as a tutor is voluntary, students should receive a thorough explanation of the program and what will be expected of them. (If tutor recruitment is done at the beginning of the school year it will require the re-assignment of students to classes so that all tutors are in the same class. The secondary school must be aware of this.)

6. *Train Tutors*. After tutors are recruited and are together as a class, they are trained for a few weeks in tutoring. (Tutor training is described later.)

7. *Conduct Tutoring*. Following tutor training, actual tutoring begins and continues for a definite time period. While tutoring goes on, the secondary school teacher and the elementary school's Tutoring Coordinator visit classrooms and assist tutors who require additional ideas or encouragement. These two teachers also supervise an elementary school class while the classroom teacher meets with tutors, gives them ideas and retraining, or solicits the tutors' ideas and problems.

8. *Evaluate and Revise*. At the completion of a tutoring cycle, an evaluation is conducted to determine the effectiveness of the program. Tutors, learners, and teachers complete brief questionnaires, which are summarized by the Tutoring Coordinator and discussed at a meeting of all involved teachers. During that meeting revisions to the program for the next tutoring cycle are agreed upon.

At the end of the school year a thorough evaluation is carried out to determine how well the interschool tutoring program has met its objectives for students in both schools. Plans are then developed for the subsequent year.

TUTORING ARRANGEMENTS

Most interschool tutoring is one-to-one, with a secondary tutor helping a single elementary learner. However, because of their maturity, secondary students often can be responsible for more than one learner, although the tutor will help them one at a time.

In some instances tutors can work with small groups of learners. The success of this arrangement is dependent on two factors: the degree of structure built into the small-group task, and the demonstrated capability of the tutor. Many tutors cannot function well as leaders of small-group instruction, and it is unwise to assume that they can because of their age (and size!). Rather, it is preferable to observe tutors in action in the one-to-one setting and decide which ones show promise as small-group leaders. When they have been discovered, it is important that the small-group tasks be carefully laid out so that tutors and learners don't meet with frustrations.

TUTOR TRAINING

Training secondary school students as tutors is relatively complex because they are physically removed from the elementary school. Therefore, much of the orientation training is conducted by the elementary school's Tutoring Coordinator.

The first step in tutor training is to have the tutors visit the elementary school. There they meet the principal and the teachers with whom they will be working, and observe in the classroom in which they will be tutoring. It is important to plan enough time for the tutors and teachers to become acquainted with each other; the teachers should be sure to let the tutors know why they believe they can use help and how they will be working together as a team.

Next, two orientation training sessions are conducted by the Tutoring Coordinator. These are the same sessions described in "Teacher Preparation and Tutor Training." The first is the Interview Project, discussed in Session II of the teachers' Workshop on tutoring (page 79). The second is "Ways to Help Younger Students Feel Important and Successful," discussed in Session IV of the Workshop (page 99).

Finally, classroom teachers meet with their tutors and provide them with training in the specific tutoring procedures they wish followed. Logistically, this is handled by having the Tutoring Coordinator and the secondary school teacher cover two classes while two elementary school teachers train tutors; tutors assigned to other classrooms can continue to observe or can find simple tasks to do in the classroom while waiting to be trained.

Must all the steps in the tutoring design be followed, or can some be omitted?

The recommended steps were developed and thoroughly tested in an actual school setting. They work. The desire to skip some steps and get going quickly should be resisted. Hurried or incomplete planning and preparation and an overworked staff spell ruin for any program. While other approaches may also work, alterations to this design should be made only for strong reasons and with careful thought for the consequences.

Who prepares all the tutoring materials?

The materials required for tutoring are not extensive. A committee of teachers designs any special tutoring materials for their school's program. An existing clerical staff should be able to duplicate the necessary notices, workshop materials, and forms under the direction of the Tutoring Coordinator. Additional help for assembly of materials or preparation of special study materials may be obtained from paraprofessionals, parent volunteers, or older students.

Why all the testing?

Parents must be able to judge whether the program is achieving its purpose. The staff must be able to judge whether their energies are being spent productively. The children must be informed when they have mastered their objectives. Testing provides this information. It identifies areas of strength and of needed improvement. The results of testing point the way to modifications in procedures and techniques that will improve the program.

Can all children be tutors?

Most children, if thoroughly trained, can be successful tutors. Only children with severe academic or social problems have difficulty—perhaps five percent of a student population. The sending teacher should treat tutoring as a valued subject, stressing the skills of human relations along with content area skills. Teachers will be pleasantly surprised at the resourcefulness of tutors in discovering ways to help their children learn.

Do all children need tutoring?

Not everyone may need tutoring but all will benefit from it. Individual attention in a hard-to-achieve skill area is bound to result in increased learning. Even the most advanced child can profit from the supportive tutoring relationship that continually rewards him for his own accomplishments and motivates him to further achievement.

What about regular class work missed by tutors?

Tutoring becomes an integral part of the curriculum, as much as English, math, or physical education. Since we do not say that a child "misses" English while he is taking physical education, we should similarly not impute any missed work to tutoring. In fact, teachers find that time spent in tutoring stimulates the tutors' desire to learn so that more can be taught to them during the rest of the day.

Can children learn as well from tutors as from adult teachers?

The tutors have not replaced the adult teacher. On the contrary, by using her insight and skills to diagnose the needs of the learners and to train the tutors, the teacher has multiplied her effectiveness in the classroom many times over. The tutors are doing some of the same things she would do if she had the time to spend with each individual child. In addition, the closeness in age allows the tutor to provide a special support by identification with the child's struggle in learning.

How are tutors assigned to learners?

Initially the two teachers pair children on the basis of a learner's instructional needs and the skills possessed by a tutor. Generally it is wise to pair children of the same sex, largely because older boys may resist tutoring girls (the converse seldom happens). Personalities of the possible pair should be considered to make sure, for example, that a strong-willed younger student is not put with a retiring older student, or that a shy younger student does not work with an abrupt older student. After a little while, tutors can suggest rearrangements themselves ("I think I can tutor him. Let me try for awhile.").

What age gap should there be between tutor and learners?

The tutor should be at least two years older than the learner. This age spread lets the older child get the satisfaction of being in charge while at the same time serving as a model the younger child can look up to. For older children who are low achievers, the academic gap should still be two years. For example, a sixth grader reading at a fourth grade level could tutor a third grader reading at a second grade level.

How much time is involved in tutoring?

At the beginning, tutoring takes place five days a week for about 30 minutes a day. Monday through Thursday are tutoring days, and Friday (at the same time) is reserved for meetings with tutors.

What will children not involved in tutoring be doing?

Although all members of both classes are fully involved in tutoring, some older and younger students may not be involved on a given day because of differences in size of the two classes or because of absences. Many tutors will simply do their own work independently. They may also observe other tutoring, using an observation form, and prepare to give feedback at a clinicing session. A younger child whose tutor is absent can work independently, work with a tutor who is also free for the day, or join another learner and his tutor.

How can time be found for the meetings necessary for planning, evaluation, and revision of the program?

Schools have dealt with this problem in various ways. Some have rearranged the current planning time available, placing all the time at the end of the school day. Others have reduced the classroom time for children in order to provide additional planning time. Other possibilities are: a minimum day scheduled at regular intervals; releasing teachers by doubling up classes for physical education; releasing teachers by having classes conducted by a teacher aide or by another teacher specializing in music or art; extra pay for teachers to work extra hours occasionally. The specific answer depends on each school's resources and constraints. One thing is clear: additional time will be necessary, especially in the first years of the program. The leadership personnel must solve this problem early in the planning phase.

When do the teachers meet with the tutors for training and clinicing?

Time to meet with the tutors regularly is vital to a successful program. Since the lower grade class is generally on a shorter schedule, the receiving teacher can use the time her class is not in school to meet with the sending class and teacher. The sending teacher may set aside a brief time each day after tutoring to discuss the tutoring session. Both teachers may have lunch together with the tutors occasionally to clinic in an informal setting. The receiving teacher can take advantage of any release time provided by a resource person, a special teacher, or the Tutoring Coordinator to meet with the sending class.

What is the role of the teacher during tutoring?

When tutoring is going on, the teacher is active. Primarily, the teacher circulates about the room to keep track of what is happening and to assist where needed. From the teacher's richer experience can come on-the-spot help to a pair of students. The teacher must be visibly a part of the tutoring; however, the teacher should not interfere nor reprimand unless a major infraction of acceptable social behavior occurs. (Detailed assistance to or re-training of tutors should be reserved for the weekly Clinic.) And one important thing the teacher does is to give frequent, honest praise and encouragement to pairs of students.

Bibliography

Bausell, R. Barker, William B. Moody, and F. Neil Walzl. "A Factorial Study of Tutoring Versus Classroom Instruction." *American Educational Research Journal*, 1972, *9*, 591-598.

Bruner, Jerome. "Toward a Sense of Community." *Saturday Review*, 1972, *55*, 62-63.

Cloward, Robert D. "Studies in Tutoring." *Journal of Experimental Education*, 1967, *36*, 14-25.

Comenius, John. *The Great Didactic*. 1896. Reprinted 1967, Russell and Russell, New York.

Gartner, Alan, Mary Kohler, and Frank Riessman. *Children Teach Children*. New York: Harper and Row, 1971.

Guthrie, James, and Edward Wynne (eds.). *New Models for American Education*. Englewood Cliffs, New Jersey: Prentice-Hall, 1971.

Harrison, Grant V. "Tutoring: A Remedy Reconsidered." *Improving Human Performance*, 1972, *1*, 1-7.

Institute for the Development of Educational Activities. *A Symposium on the Training of Teachers: Elementary School*. Dayton, Ohio: IDEA, 1972.

Klaus, David J. *Students as Teaching Resources*. Pittsburgh, Pennsylvania: American Institutes for Research, 1973.

Lippitt, Peggy. "Children Can Teach Other Children." *Instructor*, 1969, *78*, 41ff.

Lippitt, Peggy, Ronald Lippitt, and Jerome Eiseman. *Cross-Age Helping Program*. Ann Arbor, Michigan: University of Michigan Press, 1971. (Note: Several of the methods presented in *Cross-Age Helping Program* have been incorporated in the tutoring program described in this book. A school following this book will benefit from a copy of *Cross-Age Helping Program*.)

Lippitt, Ronald, and Peggy Lippitt. "Cross-Age Helpers." *NEA Journal*, 1968, *57*, 24-26.

Mager, Robert. *Preparing Instructional Objectives*. Palo Alto, California: Fearon Publishers, 1962.

Melaragno, Ralph J. "Intergrade Tutoring on a Schoolwide Basis." *Improving Human Performance*, 1972, *1*, 22-26.

Melaragno, Ralph J. "Beyond Decoding: Systematic Schoolwide Tutoring in Reading." *The Reading Teacher*, 1974, *28*, 157-160.

Melaragno, Ralph J. "The Tutorial Community." In *Children as Tutors: Theory and Research* (Vernon Allen, ed.). Madison, Wisconsin: University of Wisconsin Press, 1976.

Melaragno, Ralph J. and Gerald Newmark. "A Tutorial Community Works Toward Specified Objectives in an Elementary School." *Educational Horizons*, 1969, *48*, 33-37.

Melaragno, Ralph J., and Gerald Newmark. "A Tutorial Community Concept." In *New Models for American Education*. (James Guthrie and Edward Wynne, eds.). Englewood Cliffs, New Jersey: Prentice-Hall, 1971.

Miles, Matthew. *Change Process in the Public Schools*. (R.O. Carlson, ed.). Eugene, Oregon: Center for the Advanced Study of Educational Administration, 1965.

Myers, Donald. *Decision Making in Curriculum and Instruction*. Dayton, Ohio: Institute for the Development of Educational Activities, 1970.

Newmark, Gerald. *Schools Everyone Owns*. New York: Hart Publishers, 1976.

Niedermeyer, Fred C., and Patricia Ellis. "Remedial Reading Instruction by Trained Pupil Tutors." *Improving Human Performance*, 1971, *1*, 15-21.

Novotney, Jerrold. *The Principal and the Challenge of Change*. Dayton, Ohio: Institute for the Development of Educational Activities, 1971.

Pellegrini, Robert J., and Robert A. Hicks. "Prophecy Effects and Tutorial Instruction." *American Educational Research Journal*, 1972, *9*, 591-598.

Popham, James, and Eva Barker. *Systematic Instruction*. Englewood Cliffs, New Jersey: Prentice-Hall, 1970.

Rosenbaum, Peter S. *Peer-Mediated Instruction*. New York: Teachers College Press, 1973.

Snapp, M., T. Oakland, and F.C. Williams. "A Study of Individualized Instruction by Using Elementary School Children as Tutors." *Journal of School Psychology*, 1972, *10*, 1-8.

Thelen, Herbert. "The Human Person Defined." Paper presented at Secondary Educational Leadership Conference, St. Louis, Missouri, 1967.

Weinstein, Gerald, and Mario Fantini. *Toward Humanistic Education*. New York: Praeger Publishers, 1970.

About the Author

Ralph J. Melaragno is a leading authority on student tutoring, having devoted over eight years to research on and development of tutorial systems. He is a Senior Research Scientist at System Development Corporation (Santa Monica, California) where he specializes in instructional technology.

Dr. Melaragno has taught educational psychology and instructional technology at California State University, Los Angeles, Brigham Young University, and Nova University. He received the PhD from the University of Southern California, the MA from California State University, Los Angeles, and the BA from the University of California, Los Angeles. He is married and the father of four children attending public schools in Los Angeles.

About the Author

Ralph J. Melaragno is a leading authority on student tutoring, having devoted over eight years to research on and development of tutorial systems. He is a Senior Research Scientist at System Development Corporation (Santa Monica, California) where he specializes in instructional technology.

Dr. Melaragno has taught educational psychology and instructional technology at California State University, Los Angeles, Brigham Young University, and Nova University. He received the PhD from the University of Southern California, the MA from California State University, Los Angeles, and the BA from the University of California, Los Angeles. He is married and the father of four children attending public schools in Los Angeles.